HOW I SAVED A BANK
(With a Little Help from the Cosmos)

HOW I SAVED A BANK
(With a Little Help from the Cosmos)

Tadahiko Ito

TRANSLATED BY Deborah Iwabuchi

KODANSHA INTERNATIONAL
Tokyo • New York • London

Adapted from *Uchu ga Mikata suru Keiei* (Kodansha International, 2006) and *Uchu ga Mikata suru Ikikata* (Kodansha International, 2008) by Tadahiko Ito.

All scripture quotations are from the Good News Translation in Today's English Version-Second Edition, Copyright © 1992 by American Bible Society. Used by Permission.

Excerpts from *Light in My Darkness* by Helen Keller, revised and expanded by Ray Silverman (2nd ed.; West Chester: Chrysalis Books, 2000) are reprinted by permission of the Swedenborg Foundation.

Distributed in the United States by Kodansha America LLC, and in the United Kingdom and continental Europe by Kodansha Europe Ltd.

Published by Kodansha International Ltd., 17-14 Otowa 1-chome, Bunkyo-ku, Tokyo 112-8652.

No part of this publication may be reproduced in any form or by any means without permission in writing from the publisher.
Copyright © 2009 by Tadahiko Ito
All rights reserved. Printed in Japan.

First edition, 2009
18 17 16 15 14 13 12 11 10 9   10 9 8 7 6 5 4 3 2 1

Library of Congress Cataloging-in-Publication Data
Ito, Tadahiko, 1924-
  [Uchu ga mikata suru keiei. English]
  How I saved a bank (with a little help from the cosmos) /
Tadahiko Ito ; translated by Deborah Iwabuchi. -- 1st ed.
     p. cm.
  Includes bibliographical references.
  ISBN 978-4-7700-3105-1
  1. Success--Religious aspects. 2. Success--Religious aspects--
Christianity. 3. Success. 4. Success in business. I. Title.
  BL65.S85I8613 2009
  248.4--dc22
                                    2009000508

CONTENTS

Foreword   7

PART I | SPIRITUAL MANAGEMENT   17

CHAPTER ONE   Coincidences Turn into Opportunities   19

CHAPTER TWO   Purpose is Everything   45

PART II | THE CELESTINE LIFESTYLE   81

CHAPTER ONE   An Upside-Down Age   83

CHAPTER TWO   The Heart is Where God and Humans are Joined   105

CHAPTER THREE   The Swedenborgian Laws   127

CHAPTER FOUR   What Lives Inside You   135

CHAPTER FIVE   The Proper Use of Love   161

Translator's Note   189

FOREWORD

My name is Tadahiko Ito, and I am the chairman of the board and former president of the Kansai Urban Banking Corporation, based in Osaka, Japan. During my tenure as president, Kansai Urban went from the brink of bankruptcy to become one of the largest and most secure local banks in the country. During a period of great economic uncertainty, we went through a severe financial crisis and ended up as a stable, new type of bank, lauded for its excellence.

As a result, people began to ask me, "How did you do it? What is the secret behind your success as a leader?"

The truth is that my leadership style is guided by the values and beliefs I use in my own life. But I have never talked much about my beliefs because I was always afraid they would sound outlandish. Finally, though, I decided it was time to tell the truth about how I ran the bank—to the people around me and to anyone else interested in knowing.

This book is the result. Inscribed here are the beliefs and ideology to which I ascribe my success. What you read here may come as a great surprise. You may think it is absurd that

I see connections between running a company and the laws of the universe. You may even wonder whether I've got my head screwed on right.

But the truth is that I draw my management theories from the cosmos. I call it "Running a Business with the Universe on Your Side."

How did this come about?

As a child, I worried a great deal. No matter how much fun I was having or how comfortable I was, to me it seemed that life was unfair and full of contradictions. And no matter what I managed to accomplish, I knew that death lay in wait at the end of the road. Was there any real purpose to life? Just thinking about it made me feel empty and alone.

One day, though, everything changed. I realized that this sense of futility, for which I had no real grounds, was merely a lack of love in my own heart. Even better, I learned that my human soul would live on after the death of my physical self; that I would be once again able to meet loved ones who had passed on before me. I also came to believe there was a reason and a purpose for the life of every single person on Earth, a mission we were sent here to accomplish.

More recently, I've learned lessons from great thinkers, as well as from advances in science. These ideas have taken root as a part of my beliefs and value system, and I feel as though Heaven has opened up before me.

But in 1967 it was the doors of Sumitomo Bank (now Sumitomo Mitsui Bank) that opened up before me. And like most young bankers in Japan at the time, my career path first took me from door to door, collecting regular savings deposits from customers. Next I worked at head office on new product development and sales planning. Then I was sent to various branches to conduct sales promotional training. Eventually, Sumitomo dispatched me to work at Mazda Motor Corporation, where I stayed for four years.

Through all these assignments I spent a great deal of time working directly with people. And over the years, most of the departments and branches I was assigned to did well—to the point that colleagues began to say that some kind of luck seemed to follow me around.

I was by no means on an "elite" career course, but my superiors noticed my good track record. In 1995, I was selected as manager of the Kyoto Branch of Sumitomo Bank, a plum assignment. After that, I was named a managing director of the company. Things were looking good for me when, in 1999, I was suddenly ordered to Osaka to rebuild a Sumitomo affiliate, then known as Kansai Bank.

The late 1990s were a hard time for banks. With the bursting of the so-called "bubble economy," Japan's economic miracle ended abruptly. Kansai Bank, along with many other financial institutions, took the full brunt of this disaster: a huge burden of bad loans, mainly in real estate. And Kansai Bank was among the worst-off among local banks, suffering problems with nearly 15 percent of all its loans.

This is what came my way along with the grand title of bank president. The next seven years were filled with challenges. Astonishingly, though, Kansai Urban went from the bottom of the heap, dangerously burdened with bad debt, to the top. In 2005, we were listed on TOPIX, the Tokyo stock exchange, and ranked in its first section.

You might assume that President Ito of Kansai Urban slaved day and night to make it all happen. But I wasn't, and never have been, in the habit of working through the night, let alone on weekends. I've never railed at my employees, commanding them to work harder. In fact, people who know me are amazed that anyone with such an easygoing personality could accomplish what I have.

Kansai Urban is not the only company to have managed a successful restructuring during those difficult times. Some happy endings came about because of leaders who devoted their lives to their work—but there were many corporate warriors who had to give up and accept defeat. All the effort you can muster will not always lead you to success.

Why not? I believe people tend to focus too much on the material matters right in front of their noses. But these superficial issues—the things we can see with our eyes—are not what is important. We need to be able to look beyond them. I think that many people have trouble with work because they are too involved with it. By taking everything at face value, they lose sight of the bigger picture. And if you can't see where you're going, all the effort in the world will never get you there.

What then should we focus on? There has to be life in a company, and life in each and every job, an unswerving ideology. If, for example, your company invests in state-of-the-art technology and the latest in corporate theory, it still won't guarantee success. Without a steadfast ideology to back up all of that knowledge and technology, there will be no power to put it all together and get it moving.

What I will discuss here, though, is neither superficial nor made up. Ever since I was a young man, when I was baptized as a Christian, I have continued to build my own ideology based on the power of the cosmos, and it has served me well in my work at Sumitomo Bank and all the time I've been with Kansai Urban.

And it just so happens that the notion of having the universe on your side has broader implications than running a business. Indeed, I have used it in every aspect of my life, and I will be telling you about how that works, too.

It all begins with values, and I like to use a certain Bible verse to introduce it. "(I) saw an open door in Heaven. And the voice that sounded like a trumpet, which I heard speaking to me before, said, 'Come up here, and I will show you what must happen after this.'" (Revelation 4:1) In this passage, "open door" is a symbol of new values and truth. "An open door in Heaven" indicates the values of the new age in the twenty-first century. This verse is telling us that humankind will not be able to survive unless we shed off our old values.

Throughout history, humans have been shackled to an old value system that tells us that what we see in our world is all there is. The world we cannot see is subordinate to all of this.

I often think of the astronomer Copernicus. In an age when it was taken as fact that the universe revolved around the Earth, Copernicus dared to suggest the exact opposite. This is one dramatic example of how our judgment can be mistaken if we are limited to what we can see.

Indeed, the basis on which we live our lives is akin to the old theory of the universe spinning around the Earth. It certainly looks to us as though the Earth stands still and sun moves across the sky, but that old theory was proved wrong hundreds of years ago.

I'd like you, just like Copernicus' early adherents, to take a chance on believing what is written here. I would like you to believe, as I do, that if you act in accordance with the universe, it will always be on your side.

The universe operates under a very simple principle: it works toward the coexistence and co-prosperity of every living being. Life rooted in this world will always mean a pursuit of ephemeral pleasures, and it will always tend toward the selfish and self-centered. But if we all managed to live a life based on prosperity for the whole, it would mean a dramatic change in values, one that would turn Heaven and Earth upside down!

We are being inexorably pushed toward a paradigm shift, a new way of living. This new lifestyle with a new set of values would mean a much happier life for all of us. It would also give us the confidence to thrive in these confusing times.

If you still think of yourself as unhappy after you've finished this book, it will be proof that your values have not changed. But I hope that just becoming more attentive to the notion of a different value system will dramatically change your lifestyle.

I originally wrote two books that were published in Japan. The first book, entitled *Spiritual Management*, was the story of how I used my beliefs and value system to save a bank from collapsing. It is full of practical advice as well as words of hope and endless possibility. The second book, *Celestine Lifestyle*, goes more deeply into my own personal beliefs. After an enthusiastic response in Japan to my first book, I felt it was time to talk more about the deep faith that has supported me throughout my life. These two volumes have been edited and combined into a single volume for the English reading audience.

It is my fervent desire that you read through to the end, and allow me to share the foundation of my life with you.

In this book, you'll be reading about God and Christ. This is only because I myself am Christian. If you have no religious preferences or if you have a different religion, feel free to read the word "God" as "creator of the universe" or "Heaven."

All of us live according to a single cosmic providence. In my mind, the differences among peoples are based on differences in history, cultures, ethnic groups, and religious interpretations and understanding. But we must remember that God is always watching over all of us, not just a chosen few who share the same beliefs or culture or history. If we assume a humble attitude and go about our daily business, we will most certainly be destined for success. We experience some failures or times of discouragement, but that is only because God considers them necessary. These difficult times are merely a step toward our next success.

I will be most delighted if anyone who struggles with work or life in general finds in these pages even a little more courage. I don't expect my readers to understand or accept everything I've written, but I believe this is the right time for a book like this, and it is my fervent hope that it will expand your subconscious desire to do something positive during this age.

There is much more for us to consider in life than money, status, and honor. If you keep in mind the larger issues facing humanity, you are certain to experience a change in your value system. Your perception of difficulties and mistakes will change dramatically. You will be happier and more satisfied with your work and personal life.

✢ ✢ ✢

During the last stages of preparing this manuscript for publishing, we watched the world go through financial havoc, an event that I believe is a warning to us from our creator. We are being urged to pay closer attention to that which is invisible (our minds and hearts), and to use what we find there to change corporations and society as a whole.

I am absolutely confident that this worldwide economic chaos will bring about major changes in mental and material values. Our old, worn-out values put the economy first, and they are about to be replaced by new values that put human spirituality above all else.

If we are able to survive the pain of reworking our system of values, Earth could once more enjoy a time of prosperity, peace, and harmony. Wouldn't that be wonderful?

Tadahiko Ito
Osaka, Japan
2009

PART I
SPIRITUAL MANAGEMENT

CHAPTER
ONE

Coincidences Turn into Opportunities

The big change came on November 20, 1998.

"We're sending you to take over Kansai Bank." Toshio Morikawa, chairman of the board of Sumitomo Bank (now Mitsui Sumitomo Bank), called me in to tell me the news before making the official announcement. At the time, I was serving as a managing director, and it was a bolt from the blue, a complete surprise.

Ever since joining the bank, I had done well. I'd been blessed with supportive superiors and subordinates both, and I had thrived in the environment. Now I was in top management. I'd even been chosen to speak at the bank's twenty-fifth anniversary ceremony.

Working mainly with domestic accounts, I liked to flatter myself that I did well with difficult assignments. My work required decision-making skills based on experience. I prided myself in the feeling I had for the big picture, an ability to understand how each decision contributed to making the overall corporate machine function smoothly.

What's more, Sumitomo Bank was just about to start a wide-reaching reform of its accounts division, a job I was ready for. I couldn't understand why my boss was sending me to Kansai Bank when I was the accounts expert. Why didn't he need me at Sumitomo, and who was he planning to replace me with?

Kansai Bank, now Kansai Urban Bank, was a small, regional bank headquartered in Osaka. It had only about 1 trillion yen (or about $10 billion) in assets. Like most other regional banks in Kansai, the area surrounding Osaka, it was in turmoil as the financial world desperately struggled to survive in a failing economy. There was no guarantee Kansai Bank would survive. And indeed, in the 1990s more than a few banks fought bravely only to end up in dissolution.

Even among the smaller banks, Kansai stood out for its high proportion of bad loans, 15 percent of the total. But the enormous Sumitomo Bank, which had a hand in a number of struggling corporations, had always looked more kindly on its weaker parts than other institutions. Mazda, for example, managed to stay in business with help from Sumitomo. So once again, Sumitomo came to the rescue, investing capital in an effort to keep Kansai Bank afloat.

My boss knew he was sending me to a bank in a sad state of

affairs. When he promoted someone to a choice position, he usually did it with a smile. But Chairman Morikawa had a grim look on his face when he gave me my marching orders. I expected at least a kind word of encouragement, but he said nothing.

Before long, though, a series of coincidences led me to see this new assignment as part of my destiny. First of all, my boss had given me the news on November 20—my birthday. *Perhaps this is an omen*, I thought at the time.

Then, on January 8, 1999, Kansai Bank held an extraordinary stockholders' meeting to decide whether or not to accept support from Sumitomo. The matter was settled that day, and I was officially assigned to Kansai. It was my wife's birthday. As shareholders' meetings are usually held in June, it seemed to me that fate was sending a signal by holding that event on a special day.

And there was one more coincidence. Once I began at Kansai, I had to collect 300 million shares of stock (at 180 yen each, for a total of 58 billion yen) to begin the work of restructuring. This was completed on February 18th—which just happens to be my wedding anniversary.

With three such key events falling on days with particular significance to me, I decided that it must be more than an accident. I decided to accept this new assignment as one that I was meant to carry out. As a Christian, I accepted it as a mission from God. And that being the case, I knew God would work alongside me and help me change Kansai Bank into a wonderful financial institution.

Listening to the sound of my heart

By the time I arrived on the scene, everything that could go wrong for the bank had already gone wrong. Net profit for what would become our core business was only 4.2 billion yen (compared to 25 billion yen today), and again, 15 percent of our loans were bad. (Currently that figure is in the two percentile range.)

At first, the media were full of speculation about the bank's chances of survival. Everyone assumed the new president would have his stomach tied in knots from the pressure. Strangely, though, I didn't feel much stress. I didn't have time to worry about how it would all work out—I was full of ideas, and I began to put them into action.

Another reason I wasn't overcome with anxiety was that, from the beginning I knew if worst came to worst, Sumitomo would absorb the bank, and I could quit and take symbolic responsibility for its failure. There would be a certain amount of collective shame and embarrassment, and I knew I'd have my own share of that. But I worked under the assumption that no matter what happened, the savings of our customers would be protected.

Who knows? Maybe I was just overly optimistic. I figured I'd do what I could and if it didn't work out, well then, that might just be the way things were meant to go.

That's not to say the process was easy, though. I had a difficult job. We had lots of problems. And there was always the fear that government auditors would find us deep in the red. Amazingly, though, a solution seemed to appear no matter what came up.

Every time I felt stressed I calmed myself down by listening to a voice deep inside of me that said, "Don't worry. Everything will work out."

It never failed. Whenever I stopped to listen, we would suddenly have a breakthrough. It was as if I was being given a gentle push in the right direction. The message I heard gave me courage, and thus I was able to make my way through the worst of the crisis with a minimum of faltering.

Obey your destiny and fortune will follow

My assignment to Kansai Bank was definitely a matter of destiny, a mission from God. There were four specific instances where I was blessed with good luck that proved this to me.

The first one came in my second year with the bank, when we were able to achieve our operating goals. The goal originally set for me was a net profit of 9.5 billion yen, and this was accomplished in two years.

As we reached the last month of the fiscal year—Japanese companies close their books on March 31st—we had reached 9.8 billion yen. I had hoped to reach 10 billion yen but a jump of 200 million yen in a single month was too much to expect at such a small bank. So I was ready to settle for what we had. Then, in March, the yen dropped in value, prompting customers with foreign currency holdings to cash them in and take their profits. So we ended up at exactly 10 billion yen in net profits!

Similar things happened later, when we saw net business profits reach benchmarks of 20 billion and then 25 billion yen.

The second piece of luck was in October 2003, when we got a new building for our head office. We were in the process of merging with another bank, and finalization was set for February 2004, just a few months away. It was obvious the old head office was going to be much too small for the combined operations. Then I learned that the Osaka branch of another bank was for sale. Unfortunately, the building was part of a lot of more than twenty buildings that had been repossessed by the Resolution and Collection Corporation to pay off the bank's debts. There was no way Kansai Bank could make an offer for that much real estate.

The lot was eventually purchased by an overseas securities company. We knew the deal was in the works, and we negotiated with the securities company to buy the Osaka building. When we learned the lot had finally been sold, we waited to hear from the new owners. But the call didn't come. When we contacted them we learned the securities company had been outbid by a real estate agency. And if this had been just a normal situation, the story would have ended there.

But it just so happened that this real estate agency was one of our newest customers, and the president had already announced he was coming up from Hiroshima to pay his respects. *It can't hurt to ask*, I told myself as I got ready to meet the man.

"I don't suppose you'd let us have that property, would you?" I said after the niceties were finished.

"Fine with me!" was the answer I got.

And so it was that we were able to buy the roomy building, almost three times the size of the old one, in the center of Osaka's business district. Better yet, it is now worth three or four times the price we paid for it. Our new home office has been the catapult for other strides we have managed to make.

Our third piece of luck occurred in 2004 when we were looking for a home for our Tokyo branch. After the merger, we decided to combine the Tokyo branch offices of the two banks into one.

On one of my monthly business trips to Tokyo, the branch manager suggested that I go to a showing for a building in front of a new train station in the heart of the city. It looked good, and the deal was made on the spot. Before we knew it, we were the proud tenants of a building in a fashionable part of town. Later I realized it wasn't the sort of place a second-tier bank would usually just waltz into.

It had been a coincidence I was there for the showing. The owner must have been impressed to see the bank president on the spot. I'm pleased to report that our Tokyo office is a major part of Kansai Urban's success.

Finally, the fourth piece of luck. In April 2005, Kansai Urban was listed on TOPIX, the Tokyo stock market. We had been listed on the Osaka Stock Market, but a Tokyo listing would definitely increase our status.

To be listed on TOPIX a company must debt-free. This includes debts related to account resolution following a merger. However, listing is still possible if the company has a market value over 100 billion yen every day for an entire month. Without this, a company cannot be listed for a full fiscal year following a merger.

When two companies merge, bad debts are written off right away—which means that the books inevitably start off in the red. As our merged company had issued 459 million shares, each one had to be worth 218 yen if our market capitalization was to reach 100 billion yen. But as our stock was only worth 180 yen, I had just about given up on TOPIX.

Then Japan's banking industry took a sudden upturn. Attention turned to banks in general, and local banks in particular. Our stock price zoomed to 230 yen, and for an entire month our market cap stayed above 100 billion yen. Before we knew it, we had overcome the hurdle, and we were listed! And with a TOPIX listing our share price gained even more momentum—eventually surpassing 500 yen.

There we were. A bank that just a few years earlier had been on the brink of bankruptcy was now listed on the Tokyo Stock Exchange.

What started as a series of date-related coincidences turned into four major pieces of good luck. To me it was nothing short of divine intervention.

Work doesn't have to be hard

Looking back, even I'm impressed that I managed to save a bank so burdened with bad loans. That's probably why people often say, "It must have been a tough time for you!"

I have to admit, though, that I don't recall it being all that hard. Of course, I did my best whenever it was required, but I don't recall it being more than I could bear.

In terms of results, we set a new record, staying out of the red for seven quarters in a row. Our core business had net profits of 10 billion yen after two years, and now, seven years later, it is up to 25 billion yen. Our share price has tripled from its low point in the early 1990s and we are one of the fastest-growing banks in Japan.

I hate to brag, but it was quite an accomplishment to turn that headache of a bank into a top-class institution of its size. I'm as amazed as anyone else at what we achieved.

So, how did I manage to achieve so much and suffer so little for it? I do have a certain amount of financial knowledge and I've developed my own policies as president, but that still doesn't mean I'm capable of turning a bank around singlehandedly.

What, then, led me to success? Sure, I came to work every day and I did work hard. I had no idea what was ahead of me, so I gave it my all. But looking back, it's as if the road had been prepared for me, complete with all the tools I would need.

We who live in this world do the best we can with what we've got at any given time. We rejoice when things go well, and curse when they don't. But after things have happened, when it has all played out, don't you ever get the feeling it was all part of some carefully laid plan? All we can do is go with the flow of fate, stick with a good set of ethics, and do our best as required.

When I was first hired, I had two months of training. We trainees were required to write a statement of intent, and I clearly remember writing, "Even if I'm assigned to serve tea, my goal is to be an excellent tea server." Whatever job I was given, I intended to give it my best.

A little failure is a good thing

By the time I was a college student, I had already decided to leave my life to fate. Having focused my high school studies on science and math, I decided to study engineering at Osaka University, which was not far from where I lived. Unfortunately, though, I utterly failed the entrance exam. On the answer sheet, I put all the answers in the wrong row.

I was bitterly disappointed. But then it occurred to me: *Science might not be the right path for me.* So with very little consideration, I decided to switch to studying law. In hindsight it seems almost reckless.

My mother was a devout Christian and, through the people I knew from church, I had met a man who was a judge. That was all I had based my decision on—I thought I would like to be like him. The next year, I passed the exam for the law school at Kyoto University. (I originally planned to sit the Japanese bar exam, but I gave that up, too, when I got sick of all that studying!)

Soon after starting college, I was baptized into the Christian faith, largely influenced by my mother. And since I was still interested in science, I joined the parapsychology club. I was an enthusiastic participant, and the things I learned there turned out to be a great help to me as I tried to get Kansai Bank back on its feet.

After graduation in 1967, I was hired by Sumitomo Bank, and there were a few "coincidences" involved in that, too. I had originally been promised a job at the local electric company, and was satisfied with that prospect. One day, though, in downtown Osaka I ran into an acquaintance from Kyoto University who was trying to find Sumitomo Bank, where he was scheduled to have a job interview. I wasn't busy, so I took him there. And at the urging of yet another friend who was already there, I decided to apply. Amazingly, I was the one who was offered a job.

Now I had to decide which job to take. I went to my college advisor to discuss the matter. It just so happened that my advisor's son-in-law worked at Sumitomo Bank, and he encouraged me to go into banking. I followed my destiny where it took me and ended up as a banker.

We often hear about highly successful people who declare that they remained true to their original dreams. My experience was nothing like that. I had no idea what sort of work I wanted to do, no illusions about working my way up to branch manager or an executive post. I certainly never planned on being a bank president. The only strong notion I had was to follow where God led me and to do my best at whatever job I got.

So I went to work for Sumitomo Bank, and my first assignment was the Nishinoda Branch in Osaka. Back in those days, before the advent of the ATM, young bankers were sent out to visit customers at their homes in order to collect savings deposits and encourage them to greater thrift. Each banker was given a quota—and competition was often fierce.

That was how I started. I was the youngest one on a ten-member team, but I quickly became the top performer. This won me a dubious privilege. While my contemporaries were promoted to more attractive assignments at head office, I spent five years at various branches, riding around on a little motor scooter.

I did my job well and gave it my all, but after five years, collections can get tiring. Just as I was thinking about quitting the bank, at age twenty-eight I was finally transferred to head office. This, too, seemed Heaven-sent.

After nearly a dozen years at head office, I was dispatched to Mazda Motor Corporation in Hiroshima, where I stayed for four years. Then it was back to Osaka and the bank, this time as manager of the Dotonbori Branch.

It was 1989, the very peak of the "bubble" economy. And after years in the "real economy"—the nuts-and-bolts business of making cars—it was somehow disturbing to see so many banks focusing their resources on financial management and land speculation.

The eye of an eagle, the eye of a snake

It worked to my advantage that I didn't follow a typical "elite path." It gave me a different viewpoint. All that time spent collecting money from actual customers and watching cars being made gave me a very down-to-earth perspective. When it came to making decisions, I was able to see all the way to the beginning of any process.

There are lots of people who get overly wrapped up in every detail of their work. But what's the point of obsessing over such tiny details?

To overcome this tendency you have to look down at yourself from a higher level. Think of it in terms of "an eagle's eye and a snake's eye."

Snakes crawl along the ground, and that's their perspective. They can only see whatever is right in front of them. What's more, snakes have poor eyesight. They sense the body heat of their prey. People who act on emotions rather than reason are much the same. Like snakes, they are always on guard, fearful of what might happen next.

If you see things with an eagle eye, though, you get the

big picture. With that perspective you are less likely to go to pieces over small setbacks, less inclined to over-exult in small victories.

Of course, it is in our human nature to feel uneasy and to get discouraged. But those with eagle eyes have a better idea of their own position in the broad scheme of things, and that makes it easier for them to maintain their equilibrium. They do their best and find it easier to accept things even when they're not going well. You might even be able to see that a mistake here and there may well lead to success beyond your initial hopes. You'll come to see failure as a good fertilizer you can plow back into the ground.

This is something particularly hard for bankers to learn, and I see the results of it all the time. Something goes wrong, a debt goes unpaid, or some other small tragedy occurs, and staff come to me with tears in their eyes. This is my stock response:

"Think of it as expensive lesson and let it go. Study it carefully, and make plans so the same thing won't happen again."

What will it mean a hundred years from now?

An eagle-eye view should give you more than just a wide perspective of where you are in space. It should also give you a sense of where you are in historical time. A century from now, how will people look back on our era? We may well seem ludicrous! Future generations may say, "Look how they destroyed the environment without a second thought. Look how they fought each other!"

What we see around us today may not bother us. And yet when we look back on dark periods in history, we often think, "How barbaric!" But to those living at the time, that was just the way things were.

When we look back at the militaristic era in Japan before World War II, we may now see that Japan did horrible, violent things to neighboring Asian countries. At the time people must have felt it was all necessary to make sure Japan won the war. But how could people have possibly felt that way? It was because they were brainwashed by the age. It's something that happens in every single era of human experience.

What about our own era, then? Today, I believe brainwashing by corporations is rampant.

When people are brainwashed, they find it almost impossible to have an original thought. They find it impossible to tell right from wrong, or happiness from misery. I imagine some people see certain notions as absolute. For example, people equate wealth with glory or a big house with happiness. But this is just brainwashing on an epic scale.

It will be up to future generations to judge our era. We are too involved in the world around us to properly evaluate ourselves. So unless you are some sort of transcendental genius, how are you supposed to live? You can do it with humility.

The Bible says, "No one can enter Heaven except as a child." Only someone who artlessly absorbs everything around them will receive the amazing and wordless wisdom of Heaven that will transcend the limitations of time.

The problem is people who refuse to waver from their preconceived ideas, people who are so set in their convictions as to be delusional. I call them people who have brainwashed themselves in the values of the age.

You find people like this everywhere you go. What causes them to be like this? The answer is usually "hardship."

Some people feel that all hardship is good, that it builds character. But that is not always the case. Good hardship can help a person grow. Bad hardship just makes them hardheaded and unable to see things in different ways. A person who has suffered bad hardship can find it difficult to pull out of a brainwashed mindset.

I believe that what separates good hardship from bad is the original purpose. Let's say you go through various difficult times, and eventually become president of a company. If your main purpose behind it all was to make money and throw your weight around, the growth you achieve will be far different than if you became president because you wanted to contribute to society.

Experiencing hardship and consequent success for the sake of a bad goal will rationalize that goal. As a result, you'll consider your goal to have been a good one, and become a president who spends all his time bullying his employees and anyone else he can lay his hands on. You might have a chance to reconsider your purpose if you actually experience failure, but if you are successful, there's almost nothing that can be done for you.

But what if you have a good goal? Success will promote humility, and you'll understand that your achievements would have been impossible without the support and cooperation of the people around you. From what I've seen, presidents of smaller companies can generally be divided into these two categories.

From this, I hope you can see that experiences of hardship, success, and failure are not necessarily a measure of a person. The purpose is what is important, not the results. It is the purpose and goals for which a person lives that gradually shape his or her character.

Failure at work is usually a sign

Five years after I started at Sumitomo Bank, I was assigned to the business planning division at head office, the division that works on marketing strategy. The year after that I moved to the Tokyo office.

Sumitomo was the first Japanese bank to introduce ATM cards, and I was involved in that little piece of history. The experience helped to build my self-confidence. After that, I worked for a while in labor relations, then the Osaka accounts division. After that I was named the first assistant director of the Tokyo corporate division.

Through all these assignments, the divisions I worked in achieved dramatic upturns. And I became well known at the bank. Some people assumed I did it by cracking the whip over subordinates—but that was not the case. I don't believe in threatening people into doing something I can't do myself. Nor do I approve of setting arbitrary goals then browbeating employees into achieving them.

So how did I do it? I organized operations in ways that made it easy for everyone to work effectively. People talk about "creating a new business model." That's what I always aimed for. It is impossible to achieve a business goal until a proper model has been put into place. I liked to work on my plans until they were logical and made sense. It reminded me of when I was a teenager enjoying science in high school.

I take the same approach at Kansai Urban Bank. I learned long ago that it is impossible to achieve something by scolding people to get them to work at a furious pace. You have to start off in a logical manner. I knew that if people were doing their best and things were not working out, there had to be a problem somewhere. When something didn't work, I'd stop to think what the problem was, then devise a solution to it. This is the role of a leader. The next step is to carefully explain the solution to the staff.

When you take on a job, it is essential to set priorities. Many talented people make a mess of things by trying to do everything themselves. But when you exclude people who might help, efficiency tends to suffer.

I've always admired Abraham Lincoln, who apparently divided tasks into three categories: work he did himself, work he did with subordinates, and work he delegated.

In my business, there is never enough time, so I try to follow Lincoln's method. I put my priority on the work I do myself. And one task I focus on is the layout of bank branches. Is this surprising? I give it top priority because the branches are where we come into direct contact with our customers. What could be more important than that?

I also believe that people have their best ideas and their greatest inspiration right after the sun comes up. When the sun sets we want to relax. I like to stay in step with these natural human rhythms, so I always schedule meetings at 8:00 a.m. Banks open for business at 9:00, so I think it's better to engage in creative activities beforehand.

The role of a leader is to bring out the best in people. You can't achieve that by lecturing them on how to do their jobs—and certainly not by haranguing and threatening them. You have to support their morale.

Of course, no matter how hard we try, things don't always go well. Even if we do our best to persuade companies to borrow from us, some will still choose another bank. When this happens, I like to tell myself it wasn't meant to be and then let it go. Who knows? The "failure" may have saved us from getting involved in some messy scandal. Who knows what God saves us from?

It's the same when it comes to taking various entrance exams. I always advise people that if they fail, it just means they weren't destined for that path. That school or that company might not have been right for them, and it's just as well to be rid of it. What I do advise against is giving up before you even try. If you do your best and still don't succeed, well then, it's best to give up on that particular avenue.

I tell my staff the same thing: do your best, and if it doesn't work out, just forget about it. This may sound strange coming from top management, but to me, it is common sense.

Putting the right person in the right place

Human resources are another top priority for me: assigning people to positions at the bank. In my experience employees rarely fail to thrive because they lack motivation or ability.

The job itself and the environment are usually what determine success or failure.

We may like to think we choose our own interests, but each of us is born with a certain disposition. I have always liked to fiddle with machinery, and I imagine that this is a God-given predisposition. As a child, I took watches apart, made radios, and built model airplanes and electric trains. I believe we are all born with some sort of special ability and that these abilities are the "potential" we receive from God.

We use education to bring out our potential. The word "education" has two parts: "Edu" means "go out" and "cation" means "carry." So to "educate" means to "carry out," or to "bring out" what we have inside of us.

We don't know who first invented language, but it is clear that words contain the wisdom of people from long ago. They might even contain enlightenment from God. If more business owners understood the meaning behind the word "education," they might go about the way they train their employees differently.

Employee training is usually interpreted to mean "stuffing trainees' heads with all the information they need to know." But that's not my opinion. The key aspect of employee training is assigning workers to positions to which they are best suited and assisting them in achieving their potential. Any boss who can do this is sure to get superior results. If a company fails to do better despite training, it is rarely the employees' fault. Either the training is misdirected or management has failed to put the right person in the right place.

Education is more than mere teaching. You have to use it to draw out the potential abilities of employees. It's my job to make sure the business environment is conducive to that task.

The more we have, the more we want

One thing I believe we overvalue today is "free competition." In fact, I wonder whether we derive any real value at all from competition. Granted, it does help us stimulate and improve each other's abilities. But we humans are so greedy that the more we win the more we want to win. And too often we don't care who we have to destroy to do it.

Certainly, competition is the impetus for growth in a capitalist economy, but it has to be done right. When dog-eat-dog goes too far, it can destroy a peaceful society. If humans were capable of achieving a higher level of reasoning, they would be able to improve themselves without competition. Competition is proof that human beings are still at a low evolutionary level, one that keeps them steeped in avarice.

Which is more important, the mouth or the nose? Which is prettier, a tulip or a cherry blossom? These are not points worth competing over. We know that both body parts are important and both flowers are lovely. Humans tend to be lazy unless motivated, so they've got to compete over everything in order to get anywhere. And once they do that, they've signed the deal for discontent.

I agree that a certain amount of competition spurs self-improvement, but when people need to win for winning's sake, it becomes a problem. In business or sports or academics, winning should never be the ultimate goal. It's the same with money. Making money should be the means to an end, and never the be-all and end-all. For example, in their obsession with higher profits, some companies window-dress their accounts to manipulate the stock price.

So, what is the answer? I believe we need to find as much joy in coexistence as in competition. Show me a person who finds joy in the success of others and I'll show you someone who can be happy whether they win or lose. When they win they can savor their achievement, and when they lose they can appreciate having done their best. With this sort of attitude, you can appreciate others and their achievements and efforts. It allows you to find and share joy with the people around you.

If you always compare yourself with others you'll never be happy. If you have a condescending attitude—"too bad you came in second!"—there is no joy for anyone but yourself. You'll also notice that when you win, you will have no one to share the accomplishment with.

I believe that rejoicing with others is the way humans were meant to find joy. True human joy is savoring the joy of co-prosperity, not being a lone winner.

Unfortunately, even if you do your best to find joy with others, there will always be a few who are unhappy no matter what you do. It's a shame, but that's the way they are. Take the high road, and let them be. People almost never change the way you'd like them to.

Riding out the rough patches

No matter how hard we may try to go with the flow of fate, it is difficult to stay calm when we run up against tough problems or setbacks. How should we deal with the trials we face? Well, think of this life as a place where we learn about life, love, and knowledge. The important thing to remember is that no matter how painful an experience, it is going to be useful in the end.

If you take the view that every lesson learned is going to benefit you for eternity, even the most difficult ones should be easier to bear. Adversity is the creator's way of making you stronger and forming you into a distinctive being.

How does God, our creator, see us? I think of humans as rats trying to make our way through a labyrinth, and God as the scientist standing over us, watching.

A rat in a labyrinth zips around, running into walls—just as we do our best to make our way through life. When a rat hits a dead end, it can't turn around if the path is too narrow. So the scientist picks it up and sets it down somewhere easier for it to move.

God does the same thing for us. When we are in a state of agony too intense to bear, God sets us down in an environment that is a little better. If we keep the existence of our creator in mind, we can trust that no matter how great the trial or how unhappy we feel, in the end we will be set on a brighter path.

If you were subjected to months of overtime and found yourself in the hospital because of it, chances are you'd be overwhelmed with your misfortune. But there you'd be, with time enough to think about your life and a chance for your soul to recover from a dangerous situation.

Or you might have got in with the wrong crowd and ended up with an injury, say a broken leg, from a traffic accident. It could be the excuse you need to make some changes—in the long term it might be the best thing that could happen to you.

What's vital is to always find a positive interpretation of life, and to believe in a creator who will protect you. If you can manage that, there's a good chance you'll have some amazing experiences ahead of you.

CHAPTER
TWO

Purpose is Everything

Love doesn't rust, and it can stretch indefinitely. Christianity emphasizes "love" above all else, as in "love thy neighbor." And bankers, as we well know, handle a lot of money. Most people think that bankers are relentlessly greedy when it comes to money matters, but believe it or not, a banker's job can come surprisingly close to Christian love.

When I became president of Kansai Bank, my intent was to make it into a bank that truly contributed to society. These were the policies I laid out:

1. The pursuit of social value
2. Decisive business reform
3. Operations based on respect for everyone

I laid these out at the extraordinary shareholders meeting where it was announced that I would take over as president.

It was my first task at Kansai Bank, and I decided on this platform without consulting anyone else. "Social value" and "respect for others" sounded refreshing to me in the wake of the ultra-materialistic bubble economy. I believed that running a business required an ideology, and that carrying out that ideology was what running a business was all about.

With the bank on the verge of collapse, shortsighted half measures were not going to fix anything. The entire bank had to be rebuilt, starting at the beginning by stating the purpose for its existence.

As individuals, some of us think about what we are and how we should live, and others do not. One look will likely tell you who does which. It is the same with companies. Some are run by leaders with a purpose in mind, and others are not.

I wanted to completely reconsider the role of banks and what our mission should be. I knew that once I established the principle behind the bank and set clear goals, we could go about our business of lending and collecting money.

I believe in a process of concepts, results, and purposes. Every process begins with the purpose and works backward. There are two kinds of purposes: those from Heaven and those from Hell.

When I began working at Kansai Bank, first and foremost, I wanted to choose a purpose for it that came from Heaven. The purposes of the cosmos, those that come from Heaven, have evolved over the ages in a way that makes people happier and more settled. History has proven this. People motivated by evil will often prosper for a short period of time, but if you take a longer view, you will see that humankind has basically evolved so as to make the world a happier place to be.

So, if goals are set with the happiness of others in mind, they come from Heaven. And the power of Heaven will support their progress. As such, corporate activities must be directed toward the benefit of society if the company is to succeed in the long term.

The sad reality is that although many companies claim to be in business for the sake of society, few actually live up to their ideals. Instead, all they see is the bottom line. But I believe a company that actually does serve the best interests of society as a whole is bound to be profitable.

Without profit, of course, you can't stay in business. Healthy profits mean better pay for hardworking employees and more capital to reinvest. These are results. But if profits are the sole purpose for staying in business, a company will eventually go off course and self-destruct.

This is what happened to banks in Japan during the bubble years. We lent money to anyone if we saw a profit in it. That's how Kansai Bank ended up with an enormous pile of bad loans.

We had to get rid of that mindset if we wanted to rebuild the bank and make it work. That is why I began by making contribution to society a fundamental purpose of the bank. I had our employees focus on this goal, and we set about making every aspect of our work consistent with it.

Examining everything we did, we asked ourselves whether it actually benefited our customers and whether it was action worthy of a financial institution.

There is no value in a local bank that refuses to lend money to small companies struggling to stay afloat. In fact, that's what we should be there for—to be available to consult with our neighbors in their times of need, offer them financial support—a type of love if you will. That's the sort of thing that gives a bank social value.

To make a long story short, even when we did things the way they had always been done, our objective was brand-new. The old goal had been "making money by lending it to companies." When we changed that, the turnaround that followed came naturally.

We began to lend money with the assumption that we were helping to nurture borrowers. We thought about what we could do to get our client companies going in the right direction, and whether what we were doing contributed to the financial world as a whole.

I changed Kansai Bank with this concept: We would lend money to businesses that needed it, whether or not they had collateral. Our key concern was to see that the company had a goal, a reason for being, that pleased Heaven (coexistence and co-prosperity). If we were convinced this was the case, we trusted that the company would thrive and society as a whole would benefit from it.

The universe will support your purpose

When I say Heaven will give you the power you need and support your efforts to achieve it, you may wonder how I can say such a thing with so much confidence. It is a matter of belief in God. My religious faith compels me to focus corporate activities on making people happy.

Believing in God means believing in the existence of a creator of the universe. And believing in a creator means believing there is a purpose behind creation, which allows me to recognize that there is a purpose for my existence.

What then is God's purpose for us? It's certainly not to make us wealthy and give us lots of material goods. God's purpose is that we have mental wealth and live a happy life.

How can we achieve that? In a lifetime, humans go from a childish mentality to an adult one. Children can be happy without thinking deeply; they tend to act intuitively and artlessly. Adults, though, cannot achieve true happiness by remaining childlike. Again, though, we can achieve happiness by sharing joy and prosperity with others. This is possible even if we are poor or sick or in tragic circumstances. It's all a state of mind.

Bill Gates, former chairman of Microsoft, is a good example. He is one of the richest men in the world, has a lovely wife, and the two of them have been blessed with three children. One wonders what else a person would need to be happy.

He retired as chairman in 2008 and now devotes himself full-time to philanthropic activities. This is a true human being. Our basic happiness is in our mental state, and we find our greatest happiness in being of use to others.

Those who, like Bill Gates, seek to share happiness with others are truly in keeping with the goals of our creator. It matches the flow of the current of human evolution, and is the reason why corporate activities whose goal is sharing happiness and prosperity are bound to receive a push of support from the universe.

Clear principles are essential for work

I'm often asked about the know-how and leadership methods I used to rebuild Kansai Bank. Of course, certain techniques were critical to our accomplishment. But a collection of skills is less vital than having an unswerving principle behind it all. Specifically, it includes the three policies I mentioned in the previous chapter. No matter how much know-how or technique you have, you'll never achieve long-term success without them. You might do well for a short time, but it won't last.

We humans often get the wrong idea. We believe the reality we see in front of us is all there is to life. This is particularly true for bankers. We tend to put money at the center of our activities and get hung up on tangible realities. Then we are drawn by the allure of the material goods we see around us, and we dismiss the spiritual energy we need to lead a principled life.

It's too bad most people don't realize this is why they don't succeed in business. Even if two people have the same business plan and need the same amount of financing, the results are going to be quite different, depending on whether or not they are pursuing clear and principled goals.

As guidance from top management is essential in any enterprise, leaders need to have well-thought-out goals and strategies. Superior knowledge alone will not do the trick. By working knowledge into a strategy, we create the means to achieve results.

Leaders also need to understand that people have a finite amount of energy, and that it is their responsibility to focus that energy. If you focus the energy at your disposal and develop know-how into a sound strategy that is aimed at goals serving the common interest, you will succeed.

Downsizing for success

My three operational policies were not meant to be "shelfware"—you know, printed, bound, and put on a shelf to be forgotten. To evolve Kansai Bank into a corporation that truly existed for the good of society, we had to put them into action.

On becoming president, I took three steps to put the principles I wanted in place. I met with each of the bank's five hundred employees; I developed close-knit relationships with our clients; and I completely remodeled our branches. Let's look at each of these steps.

At the end of December 1998, as soon as it was announced that I would join Kansai Bank, I began meeting with the employees. Every day from then, straight through the New Year's holidays, I talked with as many as I could before I was formally installed as president in January. I spoke with everyone from senior management to tellers.

The usual practice for a new president is to meet only with senior executives and board members. But I saw the bank as a piece of art. And just as everyone sees a painting from a different perspective, I knew that frontline staff would have a unique perspective. I knew there had to be details and problems that only they would know about. That was the information I needed to rebuild the bank, so I had to hear it directly—especially from those who interfaced with customers. From this experience emerged one of my key policies:

"operations based on respect for everyone." It also led to our commitment to "pursuing social value."

Having spent years on the frontline with Sumitomo Bank, I found it easy to process and prioritize the problems that the employees described. Based on these interviews, I began the second task: developing close-knit relationships with our clients.

Until then, account teams had been divided up by region. But I decided to focus our teams on clients in similar types of business. This I did under the heading of "decisive business reform."

Previously, Kansai Bank had focused on lending to real estate agencies, construction companies, pachinko gaming operators, and non-bank financial institutions (NBFI). Together, these four industries accounted for 50 percent of our loans. Few of our resources were in manufacturing.

Financing real estate is a risky business in Japan because it is vulnerable to fluctuating land prices. This was one of the main reasons Kansai Bank suffered so after the bubble economy burst. And it was why I decided to divide our accounts staff by industry.

To increase the volume of business with promising enterprises we needed deeper knowledge of each business sector. Over time, as our staff gained specific knowledge in a particular sector, I knew they would develop closer relations with clients, especially smaller companies, and be able to offer help when it was needed.

The need to remodel our branches was unmistakable. By the time I arrived, Kansai Bank had cut staffing at branches and reduced spending on everything down to the lighting. Ours was not the only debt-ridden company trying to slash its way to survival, but the result was not anything likely to attract new customers—quite the opposite.

I visited every branch, and the situation was grim. The facilities looked shabby and the lights were dim. Even worse, the only branches left were those with the cheapest rent: farthest from train stations and foot traffic. No wonder we had lost so many customers!

My goal was "operations based on respect for everyone," but when I arrived there was nothing left that looked even vaguely respectable. So I quickly got down to remodeling.

These were the first key steps on the road to remaking Kansai Bank into an institution focused on the betterment of society. This is how we gradually got the bank to flow with the current of universal evolution.

Human resources in tune with the universe

I began thinking about the currents of universal evolution while I was still at Sumitomo Bank. And I used to reflect on how what I was doing at the time fit in with the current of evolution. Once that became my focus, I lost all interest in competing for advancement. When you begin to think about how to love God and love your neighbor, about how to make society happier, and about how to make family and neighbors happier, career advancement seems pretty insignificant.

I must have looked strange in the banking world, an industry where competition to get ahead can be fierce. I ended up as a top executive, but I never went out looking for that sort of a position. In my post at Kansai Bank, it was a pleasure to get the struggling bank back on its feet.

To advance in your own particular profession, I believe you need to search for the current of evolution and figure out how you can grab hold of it. Don't spend all your time on what you can see right in front of you. I believe this attitude was behind my own success.

Another problem with making personal advancement your goal in life is that it can leave you unable to tell good from evil. Advancement for its own sake will always lead to betrayal of others and harmful strategies aimed at increasing corporate profits. Your standards for making decisions will be whether or not you and the company will benefit. And this is where people get the idea that "no matter how they got it, people with money are admirable."

People who live to work tend to have this mindset, and they

are the ones for whom success is most elusive. Because their values are so distant from those of the universe as a whole, they are unable to ride the current of evolution. They may achieve a certain degree of success and advancement, but you can bet that it won't be long before they run into serious problems.

I devote about 50 percent of my life to my job, even as bank president. The other half I devote to the current of universal evolution and divine providence. First and foremost, you are yourself. Then there is the company you work for, not the other way around; your company is not what should be forming your character.

I'd like to note here that just because you manage to catch the current of evolution doesn't mean that everything will begin to run smoothly for you. Having everything work out the way you want it to as soon as you figure it all out is not always in your own best interest, nor it is always in the best interest of society.

You might call this "heavenly dispensation."

Just because you teach a child something requiring a high level of perception and intelligence doesn't mean it's in the best interests of that child. Our creator would most likely prefer that we take things one step at a time rather than getting everything done in short order. Otherwise, we would end up proud and boastful of how quickly we managed to reach the top.

I should also mention that there is no sure way of knowing at any particular time whether you are riding the current of evolution or running counter to it. Chances are that you will only be certain when you look back at it all years from now

Lending to the "right" people

At Kansai Bank, it was not too difficult to figure out what our purpose should be. To contribute to society we had to finance activities that made the world a better place. I did everything I could to bring that about.

I made it a practice to have lunch with the presidents of the companies that applied for loans, especially new clients seeking loans over 100 million yen. I wanted to find out if the president was solely focused on his own company's profit with no thought to benefiting society.

Take, for instance, real estate speculators who buy land in order to "flip" it as soon as possible. During the bubble, banks were able to make quick profits by lending to these people. But it's hard to see how this creates any social value.

To my mind, this was exactly the sort of business that works counter to the currents of universal evolution. Sure, we might profit in the short-term, but there was no way it could end up well. Even if a bank took over collateral on failed loans, it was still a risky business.

I never met the presidents of our client companies until the loan decision had already been made, so I couldn't just cancel everything if I didn't trust the person. But there were times when I came away feeling we should have no further business with some of them.

On the other hand, I also met presidents with corporate objectives that truly were in the interest of society, and recommended they be lent more in future.

These meetings were never formal interviews; I wanted my clients to feel at ease. Two or three of us would get together for an hour-and-a-half or so, and chat while eating. That was all it took to get an idea of how the client ran his or her company.

I have about two lunch meetings a week, so I meet with about one hundred companies a year. Having done this for seven years, I've had a good look at about seven hundred companies. Not many people get a chance to meet so many company presidents! I have learned a lot from them.

One thing I am sure of is that humility is the best test of character. The Bible has much to say about humility. For example:

> Jesus told this parable to people who were sure of their own goodness and despised everybody else. "Once there were two men who went up to the Temple to pray: one was a Pharisee, the other a tax collector. The Pharisee

stood apart by himself and prayed, 'I thank you, God, that I am not greedy, dishonest, or an adulterer, like everybody else. I thank you that I am not like that tax collector over there. I fast two days a week, and I give you one tenth of my income.' But the tax collector stood at a distance and would not even raise his face to Heaven, but beat on his breast and said, 'God, have pity on me, a sinner!' I tell you," said Jesus, "the tax collector, and not the Pharisee, was in the right with God when he went home. For those who make themselves great will be humbled, and those who humble themselves will be made great." (Luke 18:9-14)

This story tells us that the tax collector was truly humble. In those days, most people hated tax collectors, but this one recognized his own faults and showed true humility.

The Pharisee, on the other hand, proud of his accomplishments, was criticized for his haughtiness. The difference between humility and haughtiness is the same as the difference between the perspectives of eagles and snakes—which I mentioned earlier. Snakes only look at what is right in front of them. They crawl along on their bellies, and they let their emotions get in the way of everything they do.

When something goes well, a person with a snake's-eye view will quickly take credit for it. If, on the other hand, something fails at work, they get angry and puffed up and start blaming others. Or they fall apart and moan and groan, "That's it! I'm a failure!"

But those with an eagle's eye manage to get in sync with the currents of universal evolution, and they look at things in a completely different way. They see their mistakes as opportunities to improve themselves. With this attitude, it's easier to maintain equilibrium no matter what happens. With a positive outlook it is easier to be humble and to avoid being overly influenced by emotions.

Of course, you can never expect complete success. It's only normal to succeed sometimes and fail at others. In fact, if we always succeeded, we would never make any spiritual progress.

We've all heard the expression "every failure is a stepping stone to success." It's a good idea to think of each misstep as a task God has set before us on the path to achievement. Failure does much more for a person than success.

Compared to the infinite expanse of the universe, each of us is small, weak, and insignificant. That's why we're prone to making mistakes. If we use those experiences as opportunities to reflect on our past and build new hope for our futures, our spirits will grow and evolve.

The fine line between humility and pride

Although it may seem that there is a great difference between humility and pride, there really isn't.

Some people who toil in obscurity in their lifetimes become quite famous after they die. In Japan, Shozo Tanaka (1841–1913) was one such person. Horrified by the poisoning of workers at the Ashio copper mine, he devoted his life and a considerable fortune to the fight against metal poisoning. He is the epitome of someone whose great works went unnoticed until after his death.

Actually, few people get due credit for what they achieve while they are still around to enjoy it. It's perhaps ironic, but lack of recognition may actually be better for the soul, simply because it makes humility easier to maintain. To live humbly amid praise you must continually battle with your latent pride—which is very difficult to do. And that's why it's hard to become an effective apostle of God in this life.

Peter, one of Jesus' apostles, was a simple fisherman until he met Jesus. He left his work and family to follow Jesus until his death. Although willing to die for Jesus, when the time came Peter denied him three times. Later, realizing what he had done, Peter was filled with regret.

But Jesus, knowing how weak humans are, knew beforehand what Peter was going to do. He still commanded Peter to encourage others, because it is only after experiencing setbacks and failure that people can reflect on their actions, understand the weakness of humanity, and attain humility.

Later, the Romans persecuted Peter for evangelizing and finally sentenced him to death. Legend has it he, too, was crucified, but in an upside-down position to signify his betrayal of Christ. I wonder what might have happened if Peter had lived longer. Could he have remained humble? What if he had lived to a ripe old age, going from place to place being lauded as "Christ's favorite disciple"? Certainly some form of arrogance would have been born in his heart, and he might have died an unhappy man. Even for Peter, it was much better that he achieved fame after his death.

The Bible's last book, Revelation, foretells a final war between good and evil: Armageddon. The root of this word is "pride." It is because our proud and arrogant hearts continually bring humanity down that we will not and cannot win this final battle without God's help. And there is great danger in our pride precisely because we can conceal it all the way to Hell.

Knowing this, we shouldn't really care if we get less recognition than our peers. Instead, we should be happy in maintaining some degree of humility, and get on with the work before us.

Many people achieve fame, and with it develop arrogant pride that leads to their downfall. We see this in arrogant corporate leaders who fail to listen to advice from others. And we see similar stories in every walk of life that leads to fame.

It is extremely difficult to remain humble amid praise, so don't worry if your efforts are not recognized—just remember that problems tend to arise when we receive acknowledgment.

Leadership: Cancer cells or life forms?

In this vast universe, we are small and insignificant creatures. Every corporate leader should keep this in mind; and keep in mind that in this day and age the very existence of humanity is at risk.

It is now clear that extreme changes in climate are upon us. Enormous hurricanes hit the southern United States with increasing frequency. South Pacific islands are in danger of sinking out of sight as sea levels rise. With new evidence coming our way each day, we can no longer deny that humanity is behind these calamities. We are polluting and destroying our natural environment.

Behind these natural disasters is human egotism that is like a cancer. Cancer cells feed off the life form they live in, against all logic killing the host that sustains them. This is the way humans are treating the Earth.

We are destroying the Earth, our home, and so destroying ourselves. There is no more time to waste: we must drastically change the way we live. To do that, companies must cease functioning like tumors and instead pursue their business with humility, cooperating as a part of the global environment. I call this "life-form operations."

What can a bank do to help? We can support other companies that adopt life-form leadership and operations. And at Kansai Urban Bank we are seeking out promising new companies under the key words "new medicine/health," "new energy," "bio," "the environment," and "high tech." It is on these enterprises that we are focusing our finance and support.

Recently, we launched a support group for these venture businesses called The New Heaven and Earth Group. We encourage cooperation between established companies and start-ups with world-class techniques to promote and launch new industries.

Companies in The New Heaven and Earth Group are on track to bloom in the next few years, and I expect to see them flourish worldwide. Already, one of them is developing technology that has made its inventor a candidate for the Nobel Prize.

As bankers, our job is to support these new companies with life-form leadership. It is our way of protecting the human race and our planet. We can be certain that the companies supported by The New Heaven and Earth Group are going with the current of universal evolution. As such, although they may experience some ups and downs, I am certain that they will develop at a steady pace. And as they expand throughout the world, people will be amazed to learn that they were first supported by the Kansai Urban Bank.

Developing products using "heart vision"

I like to use the phrase "getting the universe on your side," and I don't think there is anything outrageous or illogical or complicated about it. When you think about it, it is extremely practical.

In my opinion, being conscious of the creator of the universe on some level and thinking about things in terms of spiritual concepts can yield enormous results, in banking or any other business. Right away, you begin to see your customers with fresh eyes. With spiritual concepts you can swiftly perceive what satisfies them. You can also quickly size up any company's long-term prospects.

To be a leader, you need the ability to discern and comprehend, and the measured reason required for judgment. Both of these can be honed and refined with a good spiritual backbone. They will also be evident in the way you deal with subordinates and clients. If any of them have the wrong idea about something, all you have to do is correct them. If they have a good idea, duly note and praise it. If they have problems, help them find a solution.

Those with a good spiritual backbone are able to discern the psychological condition of the people they deal with. They are quicker and more accurate than others. This is because they do not judge people just by looking them up and down. They look at people with their hearts. If your own heart is not stable and secure, it is difficult to make perceptive judgments of others.

This is what I call "heart vision."

I have seen heart vision at work in product development. In 2001, Kansai Bank became the first bank to provide housing loans 100-percent guaranteed if the borrower got cancer. This drew enormous attention and became the core of our new-product strategy.

It started when we came across a mortgage contract from a French insurance company that guaranteed 50 percent of the loan if the borrower got cancer. Several Japanese financial institutions had already signed up to offer it.

When I heard about it, I asked myself how a cancer-stricken homeowner would feel about the burden of their mortgage. Sure, I thought, a 50-percent guarantee would be comforting, but the burden would still be great. Cancer would require money for treatment, and the customer might even lose his or her job in the process. The psychological and physical burdens on the customer's family would be formidable.

Realizing this, I knew right away that a 50-percent guarantee would not do. So I insisted that we offer a 100-percent guarantee. I was able to do this because I am in the habit of thinking about things from a spiritual standpoint. And I've had a lot of practice looking at things in terms of their essence—with "heart vision." I believe this is what led to my success at Sumitomo Bank and assisted me as I rebuilt Kansai Urban Bank.

In addition, my belief in God kept me from getting despondent when things were not running smoothly. Since I knew that we are here on Earth to make mistakes and learn from them, I understood that any failures on my part would eventually be useful.

Nobody is perfect. If we were confident of our own infallibility, we would never make efforts to do anything. If we were all prophets and could see into the future, we'd never learn to think for ourselves. We have to think and strive precisely because we cannot see into the future. If we have a spiritual base to work from, we can deal with things with a humble attitude and be constant in our efforts. Anyone who can do this is sure to meet with success in some form or other.

Emotional judgments always end in failure

Let's talk about meditation, another example of how spiritual concepts are useful in work.

I get up every morning at six a.m. and meditate for thirty minutes. I began this habit when I was thirty, so I've been doing it for more than thirty years now. When I say "meditate," I don't mean that I get direct reports from God. I just empty my brain and sit quietly. It's sort of like *Zazen*. As I sit there, I get in touch with my subconscious, and I feel myself in communication with Heaven.

If you are worried or confused about your work, this is the best way to deal with it. I often get my best ideas right after I've been meditating. In fact, ideas that lead to solutions come flying into my brain. Of course, you can meditate anytime, but I find it most effective in the morning.

If I were to evaluate my level of thinking on a numerical scale, I'd say I'm normally at about five, maximum. After meditation, it's more like ten or even fifty. I have used the power of meditation to work out policies, corporate strategy, and even personnel issues. Meditation is effective because it helps calm emotions so that reason can take over. It gives you the opportunity to think of new and different approaches to what may seem an insurmountable problem. That's why it is so important for work. The more angles you can consider, the better the results you will produce. Meditation can awaken your brain and let you reason your way to new possibilities.

The opposite of "meditative thinking" is emotional behavior, or a simple person acting on the first solution that comes to mind. There is no way such behavior can work well. Processing things in an emotional way will inevitably result in failure. Human emotion is decadent. In order to set it aside and let reason take over, I highly recommend the practice of meditation.

Each morning, after thirty minutes of quiet meditation, I begin to read the Bible. Some people may think I've done enough Bible reading for a lifetime. But the Bible is so full of meaning that it always offers something new to learn. Depending on how I feel or my specific needs as I read, the meaning I get out of it can be completely different. The words of the Bible have an amazing life force.

Take, for example, the line "love your enemy." My interpretation of this has continued to change over the years. The older and more experienced you become, the more meaning you will find in the Bible passages.

Each morning, I meditate and read the Bible. These are habits that get my day started!

Do good work to elevate your soul

Why exactly do we work? Have you ever given the matter any thought? From what I can tell, most people view their jobs as something they must do to make money. This, however, is not the true purpose of work. The most important reason for work is to raise our level of spirituality.

It's important to remember that work is what we do to be of use to society. This is what I always tell my employees: "Do the best job you can. If you do, someone will notice and you'll move up in the world. But don't work just to improve your status. Do it in the service of your customers."

It goes without saying that a good business record is better than a bad one. Putting it above everything else, though, is a bad mistake. Your own record should be no more than a secondary goal. You are the only one who will be pleased with your good record. Satisfy your customers and be useful to them. If their gratitude has a positive effect on your record, then you'll both be happy.

And that's not all. When you do a good job, God will lift your soul to a higher stage where you'll be able to accomplish even more. In other words, if you create something good or do your best to be of use in society, opportunities will naturally come your way. This is true not only for bankers, but also for people who manufacture and create. I've often heard it said that some things won't sell no matter how good they are, but this is merely a short-term point of view.

How does God see people who create things of quality?

This is a valuable person who I can't afford to abandon. It would be a loss for the world.

This is how I imagine our creator thinking. The best of products might not sell in large numbers at first, but if quality is maintained and the person in charge of making them refuses to give up, such a person will succeed in the end.

It is amazing to see assistance appear for someone involved in producing something good and useful. With more than 120 million people in Japan alone, if you offer something of value, someone is sure to notice and be moved by it. Don't forget, you'll have the universe on your side!

This, of course, won't apply to people who develop products that may look good but are of poor quality. They might sell for a while, but their success will be limited.

Sure, we work to make a living for ourselves. As long as we live on Earth, we have to keep life and limb together. We have to make money, and that's all there is to it. But looking at the situation from the view of life beyond the one we have here, the meaning of work is different. Working for the sake of others keeps our souls evolving as we prepare to go on to Heaven.

Never forget that even after our bodies have returned to dust, our souls will live on. With that in mind, it makes perfect sense to work with the objective of being useful in this world for the evolution of humankind. The joy of such occupation will lead to joy at higher levels because it brings pleasure in Heaven. Being of use is a true virtue, the ultimate form of love.

The Earth we live on is the place our creator provides to practice generating the joy of being useful. Heaven, then, is a place full of the joy of being useful to humans. It is a world of wonder.

The final stage of the soul

In the preceding section I discussed how work can raise your soul to a higher level. This is an important concept because it is the ultimate purpose of life. To explain this further, let's start out by answering a few questions. First of all, what is a soul?

It can mean the same thing as "spirit." The root of "spirit" is "*spire*," or "to breathe." It represents God breathing into the lungs of humans. What comes out of the lungs are words, or "*logos*." You can say that the ability to think is the human spirit, and that feelings are shaped by thought. The souls of humans are shaped by knowledge and feelings.

The character for "soul" in Japanese is made up of two parts: one means "word," or the truth as it comes from God. The other part means "devil," and this represents human beings. We can see that our "soul" is made up of both the divine and the fallible. And since these characteristics were most likely revealed to humans by a divine source, we know that the will of God is within them.

The human soul contains both "wheat" and "chaff." Wheat yields wisdom, the positive power of thought, and good emotions. Chaff gets us thinking in a negative direction, makes use of our self-interest, and produces bad emotion.

All of us have both of these aspects within us. The difference comes in how we choose to use them. Do we use our power of thought for good or evil? The same is true for feelings and emotions. Some people use deep emotions to motivate themselves to be useful, while others steep themselves in thoughtless greed.

Still, no one is 100 percent good or bad. We all have both. The balance we maintain determines whether our souls are basically good or bad. It can be a daily battle with ourselves, and we don't always know in which direction we are tilting. If we manage to think thoughts that are true and right, we will create a noble soul for ourselves. If we live with thoughts of doing wrong, we will end up with an egotistical soul.

The workplace is an ideal place to hone and train our souls. Every company is full of evil temptation, but there is also action that leans toward the good. It's like a classroom. We are forced to practice our skills and make daily decisions that require us to distinguish good from evil.

Following corporate policy will not always mean acting for the good. If the policy is antisocial, following it will necessarily lead to bad behavior. You may be forced into one of two positions: risking your job in order to challenge your superiors for the sake of good, or protecting yourself by following the path of evil and wrongdoing. We humans always have a choice.

The choice between good and evil is not something built into our genes or decided by generations past. We are free to make our own decisions as we live each day. The record of our thoughts and behavior, and the paths we choose, are engraved upon our souls.

If the number of correct and true memories engraved within us is greater, our souls will climb to a higher stage. Even if we fail from time to time, if the mistakes we make send us in a positive direction and fill us with the desire to do better, they will help our souls on their upward path.

I wrote that the ultimate goal of humankind is to lift our souls to a higher stage, but what exactly is that? In Buddhism, it is called the merciful heart of Buddha. In Christianity, it is called the compassionate heart. The highest stage for the soul is having a merciful heart that is full of unconditional love.

The society filled with such souls is Heaven, the society of angels. It is where we aim to arrive, the ultimate purpose of our lives. But we have to fight with devils to get there. It is how we fight the battle between good and evil within ourselves, and how we build up an immunity to defeat evil.

Prioritizing joy

Heaven is a place that overflows with joy. When you hear this, what sort of place do you imagine? Perhaps you envision people taking long, relaxing afternoon naps, or souls at endless play.

I'm guessing, though, that if you've read this far, you just might realize that Heaven is a society that exists to be of use. We know this because we understand that helping others is the greatest joy there is. Happiness is not status or honor.

There is endless proof that this is true. We've seen people with more money than they could ever spend, who have all manner of status and accomplishments, and yet they are not happy. In the United States there are many examples of rich men who retire and go into philanthropic work. They don't do it to get tax breaks; they do it because they want the pure joy of being useful to their fellow humans.

There are many ways to be useful, and it depends on the essence of each individual. One can be useful to society as a whole, or a married couple may decide that they need to care for and be useful to each other. But not being useful to others creates a hole in your soul that cannot be filled. What if you lived on an uninhabited island, where food and leisure were available in abundance? How long would any of us last in such a paradise if we were all alone?

If the joy of others makes you happy, you'll never experience joy all alone. What's more, the joy of many is the joy of God.

God gives the greatest blessings to those who live for others. And this means that fortune will eventually smile on such a soul.

And if God's joy becomes your own joy, it means that what you are doing is of benefit to society as a whole. What could make you happier than that? It might seem that being happy because someone else is happy is no more than self-satisfaction, but making yourself happy and being happy because of what you have accomplished for others are two different things.

I have tried to emphasize this at the Kansai Urban Bank. There are four types of joy. In order of importance, they are (1) the joy of society, (2) the joy of our customers, (3) the joy of our company, and (4) our own personal joy.

In other words, being of use to society is a valuable form of joy. But many people have their priorities backward, putting their own desire for profit ahead of the interests of their customers or society. Such souls will have a hard time attracting guardian spirits that will encourage them forward, and the angels won't have anything to do with them either. Let's be careful to keep our priorities in the proper order.

Aligning our work with the universe

The Bible tells us that humans exist "to give God glory." This principle is the foundation of the Christian religion. What then does it mean? Humans are the embodiment of God's glory—finite humans who receive the infinite love and wisdom of God and express it outside of themselves. Although various schools of Christian thought have other interpretations, this is how I think of it.

Many evangelists believe that preaching Christianity gives glory to God, but I believe that anyone in any position doing any job is capable of it.

What is "glory," though? It means a "shining light." Light makes it possible to distinguish one thing from another; it is a symbol of human wisdom. So when someone is able to express the glory of God, it means that person has true wisdom. And true wisdom is an expression of love.

A wise person, a sage, is not merely someone with a lot of knowledge. Wisdom requires actual practice in love. A sage is not someone who understands something in his or her head; you are never wise until you put what you know into action. In other words, wisdom means having the knowledge to put love into action.

Therefore, a person who expresses the glory of God is someone who does God's will. And what is God's will? God wants to see divine love expressed on this Earth. And divine love means a desire for the happiness of all people.

Putting it all together, we might say that a person who expresses the glory of God is a person who can control the part of their heart that works in opposition to God's love, and who manages to live for the sake of God's love. You could also say that the glory of God is the expression of a heart that goes from the innocent love of a child to a heart full of pure and innocent wisdom. And if you think of the growth of a human in these terms, you may be able to see that work is one way to gain pure and innocent wisdom.

It is possible to give glory to God as a banker, a school teacher, a baker—any job at all. The main concern is not what kind of work you do, but the ideas and value system you bring to it. Humans have purposes, causes, and results, and it is the purposes that form our personalities. Someone with a bad purpose in life will be a bad person, while someone else with a good purpose is bound to be a good person.

People work for many different reasons: to maintain their lifestyle, to eat, to play, to save money. A person who has a noble goal of pleasing others and contributing to society will always have great value. And it doesn't matter what social status comes with his or her job.

It is important to note that someone who has a childish goal will remain a childish adult. Adults need to have purposes worthy of grown human beings.

When your goals are aligned with the current of universal evolution, you will be supported by an enormous amount of divine power, and you will be blessed with miraculous prosperity.

This completes the first section of the book, the story behind the story of how I used my principles and beliefs to save a bank from failure. I wonder if this was what you expected. I hope that in discussing my religious beliefs I have intrigued you and not confused you. If you learned something new and useful in this first section, much more lies ahead as you turn the page: dimensions beyond the world we know; a spiritual world; good, bad and guardian angels; and the power of Heaven and Hell.

PART II

THE CELESTINE LIFESTYLE

CHAPTER
ONE

An Upside-Down Age

Lisa Randall, the theoretical physicist, took the world by storm with her theory of cosmological inflation. She has been featured on television in the United States and Japan, and with the publication of her book, *Warped Passages: Unraveling the Mysteries of the Universe's Hidden Dimensions*, she has become a household name. A professor of physics at Harvard, she is a young member of the world's scientific elite. Going beyond physics or astronomy, her theories are profound enough to change the way we see our everyday lives.

One of the most astounding aspects of her theory is that there may be dimensions other than the three we live in. Randall says there are some natural phenomena that cannot be explained if outer space is structured within the conventional three dimensions. One example is the four basic dynamics of the physical world: gravity, electromagnetism, strong interaction, and weak interaction. Of these, gravity is many times weaker than the others, and there is no answer as to why this is. And there are many other questions that physics raises. Many of them can be explained with the introduction of the idea that there are dimensions beyond the three we know about. These are called "extra dimensions." The notion of extra dimensions has been around for a while, but Lisa Randall has offered new hypotheses that can be proven mathematically.

Until now, no one ever questioned whether all matter could be perfectly contained in three dimensions, or that all matter was derived from physical matter. If there was proof of the existence of other dimensions, matter would no longer define the universe—it would mean that it was influenced by energy from other dimensions. And this would lead, as Lisa Randall believes, to the notion that such energy was connected to the so-called Big Bang in which the universe was created.

Any previous suggestion that there might be other dimensions was dismissed as the ravings of religious fanatics. But today, bona fide scientists—highly respected physicists—are busy trying to prove their existence. We are looking at a cosmological paradigm shift in the making.

Humans have long believed only in what we could see, but now we are learning about possibilities of something invisible to us but that is essential to our existence. If it can be logically proven, everything we humans have considered common sense will be turned upside down. It will result in an enormous spiritual revolution.

The mystery of the human brain

In taking a scientific approach to extra dimensions, we will first have to deal with something else: the human brain. Although rapid advances in neuroscience have revealed wondrous insights into the human brain, there are some things we are still at a loss to understand.

One of these is the near-death experience. Conversations with people who have teetered on the border between life and death before coming back to life reveal a large number of common experiences. They speak of out-of-body experiences where they leave their bodies and then watch themselves from above.

Although such experiences have been confirmed by psychologists, their cause has yet to be determined. It's almost as if the spirit has been separated from the physical body and is watching it from another, an invisible, dimension.

An experiment conducted at the Monroe Institute in the United States found that stimulating the temporal lobes on the right and left sides of the brain will upset the balance of brain waves. Five out of ten Japanese in this experiment experienced phenomena similar to near-death experiences, as did three out of ten Americans. This could mean that the secret to entering different dimensions lies hidden in the temporal lobes.

The savant syndrome is another condition that demonstrates the amazing workings of the brain. Some people born with mental disabilities have photographic memories that enable them to perfectly remember things they have seen only once. A very few are capable of flawlessly playing piano pieces they have heard just once.

It is thought that all humans are capable of such feats, but that "locks" on our brain keep them out of our reach. Some people with certain types of mental disabilities seem to somehow "unlock" their brains to use those hidden talents.

Why then does the human body come equipped with these mental mechanisms? I often wonder, what was the original intention?

We tend to believe that we have physical bodies and that our mentality is shaped by our brain. But I see it as more logical to believe that our souls exist before our physical selves. It operates the brain, which in turn controls the body. Taking this a step further, we can say that physical matter, such as the human body, exists only in the three-dimensional world, and souls and consciousness—things without a physical presence, are free to go back and forth between this world and extra dimensions.

Sundar Singh

Extra dimensions are not a recent notion. Thinkers and religious leaders have examined the possibility through the ages using a variety of terms: the spiritual world, paradise, Heaven, Hell, and the afterworld. Personally, I suspect that brilliant thinkers and religious leaders have been able to travel freely between our three-dimensional world and higher dimensions, such as the fourth and fifth. Could that be why their ideas were able to transcend our physical world?

One such thinker was the Indian philosopher, Sundar Singh (1889–1929). During his lifetime, he was known in Europe as a holy man and even traveled to Japan. He had amazing experiences.

Born into the Sikh religion, Singh practiced meditation and prayer from an early age. In meditation, Singh was able to enter a state of rapture. When he came out of his meditative state, he writes in his memoirs, he was overcome by a feeling of extreme emptiness. When he was fourteen, his mother died, and he became emotionally unstable, unable to find a reason for living. For a while he went to a Christian mission school, but he found no answers to his problems. He eventually condemned Western religion as evil and burned his Bible.

Sundar Singh finally made a decision. If existence ended with our lives on Earth, it meant there was no God. And if God did not exist, he felt there was no hope, no reason to live. He decided to pray for a revelation from God. If it did not come, he vowed to throw himself in front of a train.

He began to pray. Suddenly, he was visited by the resurrected figure of Christ, who asked him, "How long will you deny me?" Moved by the divine presence, Singh returned to Christianity and became an evangelist, preaching the Gospel throughout the world. Everywhere he went, amazing things would happen. There are tales of how he cured the sick by laying hands on them and of a leopard drawing near but not attacking him.

If Sundar Singh had never been visited by Christ, he would have lived out his days as an ordinary person. But after that experience, he continued to meditate, and he moved freely between the physical and spiritual worlds. His memoirs describe the people he spoke to in the spiritual world.

Although contemporary accounts describe him as energetic and full of life, Singh led a solitary life. After years of travel, he made a trip into Tibet and was never heard from again.

No one can prove that Singh made visits to the spiritual world or that he talked with the dead. One finds it difficult, however, to believe that a man who achieved worldwide respect as a thinker would have made it all up. In the end, it is much more logical to believe in a world of origin, a place we cannot see, a place where we shall return when our physical bodies are dead and gone.

Emanuel Swedenborg

Sundar Singh's memoirs mention a man who he says occupies "a high place in the spiritual world." Emanuel Swedenborg, a Swede who lived from 1688 to 1771, was a scientific genius, politician, and thinker. Swedenborg had his first vision of Christ at age fifty-five, and from then until his death at eighty-four, he wrote prolifically of secrets hidden in the Bible as revealed to him by Christ. Sadly, his works were so transcendental that they were largely dismissed during his lifetime.

A century later, though, Swedenborg's works were praised by such intellectuals as Tolstoy, Dostoevsky, and Balzac; and by other leading figures such as Abraham Lincoln and Helen Keller. In Japan, Swedenborg's ideas were introduced by Buddhist leader Daisetsu Suzuki as well as the Japanese Christian writer Kanzo Uchimura.

Swedenborg promoted a form of Christianity that was so far from the mainstream that it was deemed heretical by the Church. In the United States today, though, Swedenborg is more readily accepted, both for his religious doctrine and his theories on natural science. Books about him have sold well, too.

Reading these books, it is clear Swedenborg was a prophet who looked ahead to the age we live in now. He was able to write logically and systematically about the fourth and fifth dimensions. People tend to think of the higher dimensions as the afterlife, but according to Swedenborg, our consciousness and our souls regularly go in and out of the world of higher dimensions.

If modern science proves the existence of other dimensions, the works of Swedenborg will have to be reevaluated and could become central to our understanding of spiritual existence.

Even more remarkably, within the writings of Kobodaishi Kukai, founder of the Shingon sect of Buddhism, are teachings similar to those of both Swedenborg and Sundar Singh. Research has compared the three. I imagine that all people known as "holy" or "sainted" have been enlightened by their transcendence into higher dimensions and returned from them with a superior set of values.

I am certain that the cosmos can no longer be defined as confined to a mere three dimensions. In fact, this definition is in the process of being abandoned by science and theology. Of course, this does not necessarily lead to proof of life after death or the existence of fourth and fifth dimensions.

But if we want to convince people that life is worth living, then I say that it is best done using the existence of higher dimensions. To believe that prosperity in this world is all we can aspire to is to lead a life centered on money and social status. The basis of our existence is not here, but in higher dimensions. If we believe that life continues after death, it is possible to view the world we live in from a higher vantage point. It is an opportunity for us to change our value system.

Clues to rediscovering yourself

So where do humans come from, and where do they go? One answer is that life is a combination of natural, accidental occurrences that resulted in evolution. It is beliefs like this that can make life seem empty. It would mean that you and I and everyone else just happened to be born and that once we're dead, there won't be anything left of us. What about all those years we spent in school? Was all of that meaningless? Anyone who answers that last question in the affirmative may be inclined to pursue ephemeral pleasures. Since we have lived so long with the idea that the universe is limited to three dimensions, it isn't surprising that there are so many people who act that way.

What, though, if there were a fourth and fifth dimension invisible to our eyes? Let's assume that the creator of the universe lived in those dimensions. If you knew that to be true, wouldn't that change your concept of humankind as an accidental life form that had somehow managed to make it this far on the evolutionary scale? Wouldn't it change how you thought about yourself?

If a Christian or a Jew, you would call the creator "God." There are other ways of referring to this presence, such as Heaven or Buddha. There is nothing wrong with any of these terms, and there is no need for everyone to use the same one. I myself am a Christian, so I use the term "God." In any case, if you were to discover that humankind was put on Earth by the creator of the universe for a certain purpose, it would mean making a new discovery about yourself.

If discovering yourself means discovering your creator, I think it follows to say that people who live unaware of their creator can never discover their true selves. To believe the world is limited to three dimensions is to believe that death of the physical body is the end. If we believe Sundar Singh and Swedenborg, however—if we can believe there is a spiritual world and higher dimensions—we can live in hope that our souls will live on after the demise of our physical beings.

This may seem terribly unlikely, but thousands of years ago, and even today among peoples in unexplored lands, humans were and are much more in touch with the afterworld. Ancient shamans were able to move freely in and out of such dimensions. That is why, even after the dawn of civilization, people continued to believe in life after death.

My own belief is that the senses of these ancients were much sharper than ours today. I believe they were able to feel electromagnetic waves emanating from higher dimensions, and they were much more sensitive to consciousness, emotions, and other fluctuations.

Lisa Randall's theory holds that gravity links our three dimensions to other dimensions. I imagine that it is gravity, something equivalent to electromagnetic waves, consciousness, emotions, and other fluctuations, that links our world to the world from which we come.

Other dimensions were so familiar to the ancients that they built pyramids as entrances to it, as devices to send people into the afterworld, there to lead prosperous lives.

We know the Mayans had an amazingly accurate knowledge of astronomy, and this might have grown naturally out of a link to the fourth and fifth dimensions. They must have used other words to describe them, but they likely accepted these other worlds unconsciously and instinctively.

Helen Keller

If we assume that there is a God (the creator of the universe), then we must also assume that such a God would manifest itself to the humans it had created. At the very least, the first humans would intuitively have known of God. Modern people, on the other hand, are always saying, "There is no God," or "I can't believe in God." This is because our material society has summarily freed itself of any higher power. In our pursuit of ephemeral pleasure, we have become insensitive to our creator and lost our intuitive awareness of other dimensions. There are, though, people today who are still in touch with their basic intuitions.

A good example is Helen Keller (1880–1969), a woman who overcame three major disabilities—the lack of sight, hearing and speech. In her memoirs she wrote the famous account of the day her teacher, Anne Sullivan, taught her the word for "water."

Because of Helen's disabilities, Sullivan could only communicate with her through touch. In this episode, Helen relates how her teacher did her best to teach her words through touch, but in the beginning, none of it made sense to her.

> My teacher . . . taught me the names of a number of objects. She put them into my hand, spelled their names on her fingers and helped me to form the letters; but I had not the faintest idea what I was doing. I do not know what I thought. I have only a tactile memory of my fingers going through those motions and changing from one position to another.

At this point, Helen did not yet understand the link between words and knowledge. One day, Anne Sullivan decided to teach her the word for water. She put Helen's hand into a cup of water and spelled the word w-a-t-e-r on her hand. She did it several times, but Helen kept getting the cup and water mixed up. When Helen ran out of patience, Sullivan took her outside and began pumping water out of the well so that Helen could touch it unimpeded by anything else. It was in that instant that Helen finally understood.

> With her other hand she spelled *w-a-t-e-r* emphatically. I stood still, my whole body's attention fixed on the motions of her fingers as the cool stream flowed over my hand. All at once there was a strange stir within me—a misty consciousness, a sense of something remembered. It was as if I had come back to life after being dead!
>
> I understood that what my teacher was doing with her fingers meant that the cold something that was rushing over my hand was water, and that it was possible for me to communicate with other people by these hand signs. . . . Now I see it was my mental awakening. I think it was an experience somewhat in the nature of a revelation.

This was how Helen learned that words were a method of interpersonal communication. Most people have never thought of words as mere noises or of writing as nothing more than strings of letters. We know that they have some kind of meaning. The word "mother" is not just a sound, it has in it the meaning of the person who raised us. In a world where words have no meaning and there is little more than the sense of touch, though, "mother" cannot be understood. When Helen Keller understood the meaning of words, the depth of her being was finally manifested.

Her experience was a form of proof that words are what make humans what they are. Words are used to convey knowledge, and knowledge gives humans reason. Reason put into action results in wisdom. We can therefore say that words lead to human wisdom.

Words are also the only way we have to receive the intent of our creator in higher dimensions. For me, as a Christian, the intent of our creator is communicated through the Bible. God is an infinite being who transcends time and space. But for humans, who are limited to the three-dimensional world, words are the only means we have to connect with God. Once she learned words, Helen Keller began to feel the presence of a creator.

As I noted, the acute sensibilities of ancient peoples allowed them to go to and from this life, the afterlife and higher dimensions. Modern humans have the same potential; we have no less ability to recognize God. The problem is that modern man has become more sensuous, and this has caused a regression in such powers.

Denied every sense but touch, Helen Keller was more receptive than most people to things that are not visible. Once she could understand that words enabled communication with others, she was able to go a step further toward an understanding of God. This was most likely what enabled her to understand the eclectic teachings of Swedenborg.

The existence of God and the gift of free will

God, creator of time and space, is infinite, which means that we, who do have limits, can neither see nor touch God and therefore may not be absolutely sure of the presence of our creator.

I'd like to convince you of the existence of God. First of all, I can sense God in the complicated, precise mechanisms of the universe. There are more celestial bodies than we could ever count, and the fact that they revolve in perfect order in relation to each other is no less than miraculous. Who could imagine that such a feat was an accident?

On the other hand, the DNA in the core of each living cell is packed with billions of pieces of information (base sequences), all neatly in order. I find it impossible to believe this is an accident of nature. I can feel within such perfection the existence of an almighty creator.

Other evidence is presented as NASA discovers another ultra-sophisticated, yet uniform property in space. More and more, the most logical assumption is that the universe operates under its own volition; it has a will.

The second part of my justification of a divine presence is the belief in God held by so many great persons. Without even including theologians, history is filled with great thinkers who had deep religious beliefs: Abraham Lincoln, Helen Keller, Isaac Newton, Albert Einstein—the list goes on and on. Newton and Einstein are particularly good examples because they were scientists at the vanguard of their fields. Their studies led them to believe that God was the only viable explanation for what they discovered.

Thirdly, I propose as proof the fact that God is revealed only to those who seek such a presence, and is invisible to others. The Bible says, "Happy are the pure in heart; they will see God!" (Matthew 5:8) The word "pure" indicates a child-like innocence. Such people will see God, but those with greed and avarice will not. Human material desires are obstacles to knowledge of God. To put it another way, human beings are born with certain instincts, among them the ability to know their creator.

Those who wish to maintain their childlike purity shrug off worldly desire, reflect on their impure selves and do their best to recover their innocence. When humans are humble and have a strong desire to repent their sins, they will meet the God of love who will forgive their sins and encourage them forward.

At any rate, the claim of someone who is greedy and materialistic that God does not exist offers no proof in the matter.

The face of God is hidden to humans so that it will not obstruct our free will. But when a person earnestly desires God, God is manifested before us. At the very least, it is safe to say that neither God nor Christ forces himself on us. If God were to appear with great frequency, it wouldn't be to appear to those with pure hearts (there aren't enough of them!) but to mete out punishment. If that were the case, we would be too frightened to get on with our lives. Accordingly, it is more accurate to say we are "aware" of God. We could change the Bible verse to say, "God appears to the pure in heart and to those who eagerly seek God." God lives in the hearts of such people.

In the end, it is actually impossible for a human limited by space and time to prove the existence of the infinite presence we call "God." It is the same as asking a newborn baby to understand adults. We cannot, of course, disprove the existence of a divine being. But even if knowledge and reason cannot offer undisputable proof, I believe it is possible for us to perceive God in other ways.

Big love and small love

I wrote that God appears to those who are pure in heart or to those, like Sundar Singh, who seek God with all their strength. Unfortunately, this means that most people will never know God.

God dealt with this problem by appearing to humans when divine power was most needed. This was when Christ appeared on Earth.

In those days, the Jewish people had lost sight of the teachings of the Old Testament and had lapsed into formalism. They fasted and followed laws that could be kept in a visible form, but they had lost the desire to follow the more private laws of God. When this fall had gone as far as it could, and humans had lost site of the true God, Christ appeared among them.

"Love" was Christ's message during his time in the three-dimensional world. And until his time, "love" meant either "self-love" or, at the very most, "love of your own family." Ultimately Christ gave his own life to teach others about a new kind of love.

The essence of that love was not to propel oneself comfortably through life, but to make it possible for others to live. Parents do their best to give life to their children; respect from their children gives parents life. Christ taught us a selfless love that allows people around us to live.

In an age where "an eye for an eye, a tooth for a tooth" was law, Christ preached, "love your enemy" and "pray for those who seek to do you evil." In the history of the world, no one else has ever had a love as great as Christ.

We could even say that humankind never knew what true love was until the coming of Christ. By choosing death on the cross, Christ taught us the love of forgiveness and changed a declining human society into a more loving one.

We think of God as a creator, but the essence of God is more like the sun—love in its purest form—that gives everything life. This all means that when God is revealed in the three-dimensional world, it is usually in the form of acts and teachings of love.

Misfortune comes when Heaven and Earth are out of sync
Next, let's take a look at the modern age and all of its problems. The environment is being destroyed on a global scale, humanity is beleaguered by natural disasters and famine, and suicidal terrorism is rife. At home, we have dysfunctional families and increasingly barbaric crimes. The human race faces a crisis of epic proportions much worse than the one Christ was born into over two thousand years ago.

I see the misalignment of Heaven and Earth as the cause of this disastrous scenario. Heaven is doing everything it can to give life, while humans are sacrificing it for the sake of their own egos. This sort of situation is the root of all human misfortune. If we continue this way, the Earth will be destroyed in interminable competition and war.

Our values have been turned upside down. It is time to remember what our creator taught us: to live means giving life to others so that we ourselves may live.

In ancient times, Heaven and Earth were connected and early humans were able to go freely between them. The existence of God and the afterlife were familiar; there was no mystery in them.

However, as the story of Adam and Eve in paradise tells us, egos were developed when humans ate the fruit from the tree of Knowledge of Good and Evil.

As the ego of humanity grew, the separation of God and humanity became inevitable. It was not, however, a completely bad situation. When God was closer to humankind, we were childlike in our relationship with the divine force. The innocent mind of a child is, of course, a valuable thing. But if humankind had remained in that innocent state, we never would have reached the present age without growing in wisdom and intellect. Without an ability to fight evil, humans would have long ago succumbed to it.

Considering this, the upending of Heaven and Earth may have been a necessary process. Humans never would have evolved and become resilient if they had remained innocent and pure. Separation was the will of God. Only by falling to Earth could we learn the true meaning of Heaven.

Before we take on the adult values of living to help others

live, we go through a period of rebelliousness in our youth. In other words, we have no choice but to go through a time when we live only to satisfy ourselves—when we are unable to consider others. In the same way, in order to realize how wonderful Heaven is, humankind must live through a period of separation from it. Now, though, we are at the point where the period of separation has reached its limits.

What will happen next? That is what this book will strive to explain.

CHAPTER
TWO

The Heart is Where God and Humans are Joined

The relationship between God and humanity is similar to that between the sun and plant life. When the heat and light of the sun shines on vegetation, chlorophyll facilitates photosynthesis, and this is transformed into growing plants. Plants, in turn, absorb carbon dioxide, purifying the oxygen in the air as well as providing food for other life forms. The color green is testimony to the unity between the sun and plant life. When the sun is blocked, though, there is no photosynthesis.

Without the love and wisdom of Heaven, humans cannot thrive. Avarice is what blocks it. This is why all religious thought is geared toward bringing Heaven and Earth closer together. Egotistical greed would recede, and humans would find unity with God through a desire to help others live. The benefit of others would become their joy.

I've heard that the Chinese character for "Buddha" originated in the meaning "getting rid of the human." The vocation of one's ego is lost through prayers to Buddha. The final goal is unity with one's true self.

Hinduism has a well-known form of training called "yoga." I've even done it myself. Yoga aims to bring the practitioner into unity with God. Nowadays, yoga is considered a form of exercise to promote health and beauty, but it originated as a method of breathing that would awake the inner deity to bring oneself into unity with God.

There are certain Shinto ceremonies, such as *koshin, norito*, and *shoshin*, that are said to put humans in direct contact with Heaven. Koshin calls the divine presence down to Earth, norito are the prayers offered, and shoshin sends God back to Heaven.

The six-pointed Star of David of the Jewish religion, the predecessor of Christianity, is a combination of two triangles. One theory is that $\triangledown$ represents Heaven, and $\triangle$ is humankind looking toward Heaven. In Japanese, "New Testament" and "Old Testament" are translated as "New Contract" and "Old Contract." In essence both parts of the Bible are contracts or promises that seek to bind God to humans.

Christians also speak of the human heart as the "temple of God." People become children of God when they hold God in their hearts. It is, in other words, the place where humans and God meet and are joined.

The Latin root of the word "religion" has the meaning of "back-bind," or "rebinding." Religion, therefore, is used to bring humans back into contact with Heaven. If there is indeed a creator, this creator will naturally want a loving relationship with its creations—humans. Loving parents want their children to lead a free and independent life; they understand separation is inevitable. Parents fervently hope, though, that someday children will realize the great depth of love they were raised with and return to them as mature adults.

Heaven and Earth are in a similar relationship, and religion is what binds us together.

Christianity holds that there have been two occasions when the path between Heaven and Earth was open. On both occasions, the distance between the two was vast, and the upside-down existence of Earth had reached its limit. The first time is described in the Old Testament, the age in which God revealed the Ten Commandments to Moses on Mt. Sinai.

Moses was ordered by God to free the Jews from slavery under Pharaoh in Egypt. In that era, as Egypt had the most advanced civilization, it represented the avarice of humans. God indicated his displeasure through many miracles worked to free the slaves.

After the Jews escaped from slavery, the path between Heaven and Earth was opened and the Ten Commandments were revealed to Moses.

The second time the path was opened was during the life of Christ. Once more humankind had fallen into a life of sensual greed. The rules of Moses were followed in a superficial manner. The laws of God were like a fleshless skeleton, the love of God was forsaken, society deteriorated, and humans were separated from God.

This was when Christ arrived on the scene to explain the true meaning of love. By choosing to die on the cross, he taught love and forgiveness. Bringing with him the new laws of God and his teachings of loving one's neighbor, the path from Earth to Heaven was once more open.

Despite the extra chance God gave us, here we are again. Once more much of society is interested only in increasing material wealth at the expense of nature and the rest of society. Civilization is at the very brink of extinction.

Advances in science have led to rejection of God's existence. Christians have splintered into countless denominations, many of which find it impossible to coexist. The power of love in churches continues to wane.

As the world becomes more disordered, I get the feeling we are close to the next direct connection between Heaven and Earth. I believe God will make this third coming a strong one—one that will defy further separation. The Christian religion has long believed in the "Second Coming" of Christ, and I believe it is close at hand.

Where does life come from?

The Chinese character for "life" is made up of the character for "mouth" and "zero." Mouth comes from the receptacle for God's teachings, and "zero" is a symbolic character showing a person wearing a hat, on his knees in a pose of humble supplication to God. The ancient Chinese most likely had the idea that life was the act of receiving and acting on messages from Heaven. It is also interesting to note that the English word "spirit" comes from the root word "*spire,*" meaning "to breathe on." According to the Bible, God took clay and molded it in the form of a man. The man was given a soul after God breathed on him. The proximity of these two examples may be a coincidence, but I think it far more logical that ancient humans were much more sensitive to the presence of God; thus language evolved together with God's teachings.

What these two examples have in common is the notion that, even though we humans feel that we are living under our own power, we are actually given life and are made to live. In other words, standing right behind us is the God of Heaven, who keeps us alive and on Earth for some purpose.

This reminds me of "the structure of the universe" discussed in the beginning of Part II. I talked about the hypothetical existence of fourth and fifth dimensions which are invisible to us, but which are the origin of life on Earth as explained using theories of modern physics and neuroscience.

Although it may seem new to us, there is a chance that ancient humans already knew all about it.

According to Swedenborg, our physical bodies live in the three-dimensional world, but there is a different world of souls and consciousness, and they travel back and forth to higher dimensions where they receive currents that control them. It could very well be that life in our world is a reflection of what goes on in the fourth and fifth dimensions.

Think of the three-dimensional world as a television designed to receive signals from the higher dimensions. We spend our days watching this three-dimensional TV, but we never see what is going on behind the scenes, even though that is where the essence of our lives—our souls and consciousness—originate.

Since modern humans tend to believe only what they can see, they operate under the illusion that they live self-motivated and self-powered lives. When all of us realize that we are alive on Earth at the pleasure of a higher purpose, the basic consciousness of human life will certainly change.

The universe evolves for a purpose

We know we are alive because we have a pulse and feelings and sensations. But life doesn't start until there is some kind of stimulus from outside. In other words, life is a reaction to some kind of action. Knowing this, we can say that the universe, the natural world, animals, and plants, are all living beings created by some fundamental force.

One good example is the Big Bang, the beginning of the universe. Theory says that the Big Bang was a spontaneous event, but so far no one has been able to offer a logical explanation as to why and how it all happened. Where could such energy have come from?

If the universe did not exist beforehand, there would have been no surface area or volume. It is therefore difficult to believe that energy could have come from within. It had to have been a reaction to a force from the outside. I believe it is more logical to recognize that the source of the movement came from another dimension, and it was instigated by God, the creator of the universe.

According to recent neutrino research, the one hundred or so elements required to form everything were present at creation. Isn't that amazing? It means that the universe came prepared with all that was needed to form stars, planets, and everything else. As these cosmic bodies continue to form, the universe continues to grow and expand. Earth and all of the stars move together in perfect precision according to the laws of gravity and centrifugal force.

Considered in terms of both time and space, as the universe grows and develops as a life form, it also appears to be moving inexorably towards a goal. You could say it was heading toward some kind of eternal goal.

Humans are receptacles for love and wisdom

I wrote that life is given to humans with a purpose. But to us, it may seem that we act on our own initiative and live under our own power. So you might wonder why I say that we "are given life."

In the Bible, in Genesis, it says that God created humans in God's own image, God's own likeness. If you take this at face value, it means only that we look like God. On a deeper level, though, we can interpret it to mean "God, as the only true source of life, gave humans life similar to that of God—life that can be lived on its own. In other words, God gave humans life that appears to be independent." This is something we need to realize. And we need to understand that this is one of the greatest forms of grace, a gift.

Let's say you did a good deed. You must not misunderstand it as something you managed alone. It only looks that way; and you must never feel it was you alone who did it. You must understand that a great wisdom put you into action—the grace of God. Unless we understand this, human beings become proud. If pride is left unchecked, humans eventually believe they themselves are God and have the power to control others. This is the source of all evil and wrongdoing.

Why then does God give us life? As long as we receive the love and wisdom of God as creatures of his making, there will be value in our existence. The love and wisdom of God give mortal humans the eternal aspects of God. As I've noted, the third dimension is like a TV that receives scenes from higher dimensions. The love and wisdom of God are also projected through us, and this is manifested in our behavior. You could say that humans are handsets for the communication of God's love and wisdom.

God created humans to serve as a mortal version of God's infinite love and wisdom; we are a form of life that resembles God, so we need to have the appearance of living under our own steam. We have bodies to serve as an exterior, and eyes to look at things with love. Our ears are made to listen with goodwill, our mouth to speak gently and with affection. Our hands are for helping those around us, and our legs were made to take us to those who need us. We were given hearts so that we may love others.

It is said that humans are the ultimate primate. We can call ourselves the greatest work of the natural world. We are certainly the only living beings on Earth who have consciousness and souls that can go back and forth into other dimensions.

What separates humans from other animals?

In order to give humans free will, God gave us two mental abilities animals do not have. One is the ability to think and make decisions; the other is the motivation to put those thoughts into action. Animals are basically programmed to survive by following their instincts. We are human because we can think, and then put our will into action.

Here, too, we have to understand that we *look* as though we have free will. The source of what we think and do is actually God. The wisdom and love of God are communicated using humans as mere receivers. They well up inside us as if they originated there.

The two acts, thinking and will, clearly come from the left and right sides of the brain. Both neurology and medical science show that the right side of the brain is in charge of will and action, what we might refer to these days as "analog" functions. The left side of the brain manages logical thought, more of a "digital" sort of function.

What then puts both the right and left sides of the brain to work? God's image is true wisdom, and God's likeness is certainly unconditional love. God's auras are communicated from higher dimensions to us, as through an enormous TV, to give energy to humans. God's wisdom lives in the left side of our brain as the ability to think, while God's love lives in the right side as will and the power to act.

We could say that the source of human mentality is in our ability to think and act. The source of our physical existence is the ability to breathe with our lungs and circulate blood pumped by our heart. If either of these functions ceased, our physical life would be over and we would be dead. In the same way, if we can no longer think or act, our human mentality will have lost its life.

We can think of God's love and wisdom as being sent to humans to give them energy in the same way the sun sends energy to Earth in the form of heat and light so that plants and animals can live. The only difference among us all is that humans have free will, and for that reason human life is unable to live by the natural and orderly laws of nature. For better or for worse, therein lies the history of human beings.

It is interesting to me that the English word for "human" derives from *hum*, which means "soil." The name "Adam" of Adam and Eve also means "soil." It makes me think of light and heat coming down from Heaven to nurture seeds of plants. It is just like God sending down wisdom and love to humans to give them mentality and DNA so they can be nurtured and grow.

We can also think of God's word as seeds; and we know that God's words are the truth. In other words, the appellation "human" symbolizes the act of learning the truth and living by it.

Just as soil devoid of seeds is barren, the soul without truth is unable to grow. It is only after grasping the truth that we become human. The ancients also seemed to understand the importance of learning and accepting truth when they developed the word "human."

Discovering truth

According to the Bible, Christ left many wise words behind for his disciples before he died on the cross. Some of them were on the subject of eternal life: "Eternal life means to know you, the only true God, and to know Jesus Christ, whom you sent" (John 17:3).

These were actually words spoken by Christ in reference to God his father. He was referring to humans. It means that eternal life begins with knowing the truth. When a person puts truth into action, it becomes his or her life, making it an eternal one. In order to obtain eternal life, one must obtain the wisdom of our creator, the God of love, as well as the wisdom of Christ, who showed the way for sinners to become children of God.

The Bible says, "A healthy tree bears good fruit, but a poor tree bears bad fruit. A healthy tree cannot bear bad fruit, and a poor tree cannot bear good fruit" (Matthew 7:17-18). In this verse, "a healthy tree" represents correct understanding (truth), and "good fruit" is an expression of affection. In other words, if knowledge is mistaken, one is unable to obtain true power of reasoning (conscience) or wisdom. This will make it impossible to know what true love is.

We have got to sort out the knowledge we have and separate that which is true from that which is not true; namely, we need to separate the knowledge of Heaven from that of this world. Only those who have a great deal of the knowledge of truth as revealed by Heaven for the sake of eternal life will be able to act as receptacles of God's love—because only they are able to truly love their neighbors.

The greater the knowledge we humans have, the greater our ability to change. High-level knowledge means high-level reasoning and conscience—and a higher level of love and affection. The highest level of this love is the joy of prospering together with others, and celebrating and sharing their happiness.

A person may be satisfied to be artless and pure, but such simplicity can be easily broken and it begins and ends with itself. This is not a bad thing, but God aims for higher growth and the pursuit of immortality.

Humanity reaches a turning point

As Christ taught us when he preached about loving one's neighbor, we must have the correct knowledge and know truth if we are to be filled with the eternal love of God. Unfortunately, our ancestors have a record of mistaken knowledge and customs that prevented this. Misdirected knowledge produces the wrong sort of love, and it is imprinted on us in the form of genes. We can make some hypotheses about the wiring of the nerves and generation of other material (neurotransmitters) in our brains.

It has been two thousand years since Christ lived on Earth, and more thousands of years since the beginning of civilization. The brains of modern humans are likely filled with the resentments and hatred of our ancestors. There are many different kinds of matter in the brain, but some are present in excessive amounts and they produce excessive amounts of genes, which appear in the form of feelings that strive to vent the desire to hate and kill.

In all parts of the world we hear about murders committed by children. In Japan, a young girl murdered a friend who she heard had spoken ill of her. The girl stabbed her friend and then waited there for her to die. This is terrifying behavior. Most children that age would exhibit greater emotion in such a situation. What could have driven the girl to do such a thing? I believe that the desires and behavior of ancestors who needed to vent their hatred or settle a grudge must be passed on as genes, where they reappear when the circumstances are right. It is the only possible explanation.

God gave humans free will, including the freedom to do wrong. These wrongful thoughts and deeds have built up over thousands of years, until in this modern day and age they have probably reached a dangerous peak. That is how I see it. Couldn't it be the reason for all of the frightening crimes that have been committed over the past decade or so?

Perhaps in decades to come, these genetic tendencies will jeopardize the very existence of humanity and our world. If this happens, I am certain the creator of the universe will take action to stop the evil we have wrought. Heaven and Earth will once again be joined, and the twenty-first century will see a renaissance of human life. People will finally understand why God created the Earth and the true meaning of human life. They will receive God's energy at its source and the ability to use it.

It is said that humans only use about 3 percent of their brain capacity. In the new age, human capacity will reach a level that we cannot even imagine right now.

The past evils of humanity will serve as lessons for the new age and make us stronger for the sake of doing good. It will be like the Othello game where the winner turns the chips over and changes their color. The evil side of the chips will be flipped over to the good sides. Again, based on experience, knowledge will be integrated with reason to create true wisdom. This wisdom will be used to print human genes with a deep love and affection for one another.

Evolving "common sense"

This book is no more than my own ideas on life. Right now, I believe it to be the right way to think and live, and I know there are plenty of people who will not believe it or agree with me. Since it describes a faith quite different from conventional Christianity, many people will find it confusing. But I believe it is logical.

Faith is reason (conscience) based on truth. Faith without reason is merely blind acceptance. And religious wars throughout history show how blind belief wreaks destruction. I've been surprised to hear many believers of different religions say, "I believe because I don't understand" or "my belief is beyond logic." One should never believe anything that is illogical. Although miracles are a key aspect of many religions, you shouldn't believe just because something is miraculous. Even evil spirits can work miracles.

The auras of God's love and wisdom do not originate in the world of three dimensions, so it is impossible to provide material proof. It is as difficult as trying to prove exactly what a mother's love is. How then can we decide whether or not something is logical? We need deep knowledge and reason and a heart that loves the truth in order to pursue it. God sends us the power to understand the truth and to love what is true. We must avoid believing just so others will see us in a favorable light or because it is advantageous. This is no more than looking for a quick profit.

Galileo is one who pursued the truth. Even when he yielded to the court of the Church, he mumbled, "But I still believe the Earth turns on its axis." We are impressed that Galileo stuck to his beliefs, but there is also a lesson to be learned here: history has not been kind to the authorities who believed the Earth was the center of the universe (the Ptolemaic theory) and refused to humbly consider the notion that the Earth could possibly rotate around the sun as part of the solar system (heliocentrism).

Modern science considers those ancient people fools. In this modern day and age there is conclusive proof that the Earth revolves around the sun. To us, it is common sense.

Galileo was eventually proved correct, but in those days, the Ptolemaic theory was common sense. You could say that the latter was "correct" the way things are perceived in the mind of a child, while the former required more mature reasoning and understanding. It was a matter of whether or not you were capable of imagining something you could not see with your own eyes. Even nowadays, "common sense" is not always ultimately right.

For this reason, it is vital that we always have in the corner of our minds the notion that what is considered true and correct right now might suddenly change. You should never consider the current idea of "right" to be an absolute. Ten years from now, a theory newer than that of Lisa Randall may be discovered and everything I've written here will be superseded.

Isaac Newton, who discovered the law of gravity, said "I was like a boy playing on the seashore, and diverting myself now and then finding a smoother pebble or a prettier shell than ordinary, whilst the great ocean of truth lay all undiscovered before me." In my mind, this is the perception of a righteous man. We have to begin with the notion that there is a limit to what humans know, and there are only a few things we are equipped to pass judgment on.

Once we know that, we can do our best to gain knowledge and reason. The method for good is to decide what seems logical to you. But what you consider good at this moment may only be true for a short time. If you believe yourself to be absolutely correct, you will fall into a trap. No just human being will ever consider his or her "common sense" to be absolute. We must always remember that all thoughts are constantly liable to revision.

Humans must develop and grow, eternally adding to our wisdom. We must confront truth with humility.

Joy and suffering: We have a choice

What exactly is the human heart? Sometimes it is healthy, and other times it is in poor shape. Amazingly, the Bible refers to the heart as "the temple of God." It means that, with God in our hearts, we are children of God. The human heart is where God becomes manifest to us and where God joins together with us. In other words, anyone can create a "kingdom of God" in his or her heart.

This is what the Bible has to say about it:

> Some Pharisees asked Jesus when the Kingdom of God would come. His answer was, "The Kingdom of God does not come in such a way as to be seen. No one will say, 'Look here it is!' or, 'There it is!'; because the Kingdom of God is within you." (Luke 17:20-21)

We may believe that we control our own hearts, including our decisions and emotions. You could almost say that we consider ourselves rulers of the kingdom we call our own heart. But the Bible says differently. No matter how free we may appear to be, the will of God, creator of the universe, is hard at work. The Bible says that the heart is the place where "the love and wisdom of God" reside.

If the heart is our inner kingdom, the things that happen outside of us are an outer kingdom. It might seem natural to consider what is inside you as separate from what is happening around you in the outside world. In fact, however, the inside world and the outside world are mirror images of each other. The outside is an expression of the inside. We use our inside eyes to view the outside, and the outside world can appear very differently to each of us. Some may view a scene as unpleasant while others may find it enjoyable.

Depending on whether correct rules and values are in place in the inner kingdom, the outer world can be either barbaric or full of judgment, or it can be full of love. For example, when there is greed inside, it generates an outward expression of avarice and has an adverse effect on the outer world. We tend to look for the causes of problems in the outside world, but it may just as well be a basic problem from inside ourselves.

To be a person with a large receptacle for love and to always have enough to lavish generously on others, we must perfect the kingdom inside ourselves. When it becomes a home for the love and wisdom of God, it will eventually change the way you deal with people out in the world. You could say that how you nurture yourself inside will either improve or have a detrimental effect on the world outside you.

We have seen how the exact same situation can make some people happy and others miserable. What determines which it will be? I believe it is individual knowledge and experience.

Some people may dream of a self-sufficient lifestyle in the mountains. To others, though, the thought of planting seeds, pulling weeds, and collecting rainwater may sound like a life of poverty. I assume that people who choose such a lifestyle find it fulfilling. In other words, one's knowledge is the material from which the kingdom of the heart is made. And the best knowledge you can achieve is "the love and wisdom of God." Before completing and perfecting the outside world, we must first each build our own kingdom of God in our hearts. It is the foundation of human happiness.

CHAPTER
THREE

The Swedenborgian Laws

It may seem odd to talk about the existence of a spiritual world—and many people would reject this notion. If, however, we get proof of other dimensions, it will be impossible to deny the presence of spirits, a subject of discussion for thousands of years.

In the Bible, Christ frequently confronts spirits. He doesn't speak of them as symbolic; he speaks of angels and spirits from the fourth dimension as being in close connection to this world. And many prominent, rational people have spoken publicly of the existence of spirits, in both this and past ages. So it might actually be more logical to assume that there *is* a spiritual world.

When I was a college student, I belonged to the parapsychology club. In those days, parapsychology was a bona fide field of study pursued by scholars at both Harvard and Moscow State University. The idea was that there was a mental state even deeper than conventional psychology had identified, and parapsychology was the pursuit of it. While in the club, I read a number of books on the subject. The ones I considered most reliable (and still do!) were *Visions of the Spiritual World* by Sundar Singh and *Heaven and Hell* by Emanuel Swedenborg.

According to both Singh and Swedenborg, even though our physical bodies are in the world of three dimensions, our spirits travel beyond it to the fourth and fifth dimensions. Swedenborg wrote about the laws of the spiritual world as revealed to him by God.

In the Bible, Christ spoke about how the time was not yet right to speak of Heaven.

> You do not believe me when I tell you about the things of this world; how will you ever believe me, then, when I tell you about the things of Heaven? And no one has ever gone up to Heaven except the Son of Man, who came down from Heaven." (John 3:12-13)

The time came in 1741, when God appeared to the scientist Swedenborg, and, over thirteen years, let him observe the worlds of the afterlife and left him with enough information for an enormous book. The writings of Swedenborg are so systematic that it is impossible to believe that he made it up.

In his day, Swedenborg was rejected by the Church, but I believe that his writings are logical and true. I'd like to introduce five simple rules that are of great interest.

The Law of Three Worlds

Swedenborg spoke of the three worlds of the afterlife: Heaven (of which there are several), the Spiritual World, and Hell (also in multiplicity). Spirits and angels inhabit these realms after their physical bodies die. Heaven is where people who become children of God go to live. Hell is where people go to be rehabilitated. The Spiritual World, or the fourth dimension is a kind of middle ground between the two. The fourth dimension is for God's creations, and the fifth dimension is the world of God. The world we live in is linked to the Spiritual World, which is also influenced by what happens in Heaven and Hell.

When a person dies, spirits hold court and decide whether to send the soul to a Hell or the Spiritual World. Very few go directly to Heaven. Hell is for those who spent their lives nursing especially strong avarice. In Hell, spirits go through rigorous training before being sent to the Spiritual World.

It is important to note here that souls go to the places for which they have prepared themselves. Those who, on Earth, delighted in the divine love for their neighbors go to Heaven.

Those who engaged in a hellish self-love go to Hell. Even in the Spiritual World, souls who make the grade may go to Heaven to train further among spirits and angels.

There are three Heavens. First is The World of Knowledge: Effect. The second is The World of Reason: Concept. The third Heaven is The World of Wisdom: Purpose. At each level, souls are taught by angels as they continue their upward path. Since this is the sort of system the afterlife runs on, even souls sent to Hell have every possibility of rising higher, although it might take thousands or millions or billions of years. It may sound like a long time, but not when you consider the time that has passed since the universe was created and the fact that it will continue into eternity.

The Law of Heavenly Inflow

Just as the light and warmth of the sun fall to Earth, so does energy from the love and wisdom of God fall from Heaven onto the Spiritual World. It is the energy of love which commands us to "coexist!" Wisdom works to bring about that possibility. This energy goes from the angels of Heaven to the good spirits in the Spiritual World, and eventually down to Earth to influence us humans. This becomes our own knowledge and wisdom—the source of life.

Just as the sun shines on all of us, so the outflow from

Heaven falls on all humans, good and bad alike. Each individual, however, can only receive as much as his or her spiritual nature will allow. On the other hand, Hell also makes approaches to human beings. These approaches stimulate the evil and fallaciousness inside us.

The outflow of energy from God to humans was experienced by the innocent ancients as love; a real, emotional feeling. They were also able to clearly hear the wisdom of God as words. In this modern age where humans have lost their connection to God, the profound feeling of love is only rarely experienced. Wisdom, too, comes to us although we never understand from where. We listen to God's wisdom and call it our good conscience.

As humans have evolved and matured, it has become more and more difficult to hear that voice within us, but it is there, and whoever listens for it with a humble heart will be able to hear it.

The Law of Freedom in Equilibrium

Human souls are positioned between Heaven and Hell, and they are free to accept the approaches of both. It is not as simple as merely accepting the good based on heavenly inflow. If the approach of good is too forceful, we may feel as though we have lost our freedom. If we are overcome by evil, we may feel that we have no choice but to do evil, and that can be frightening. This is why humans are placed in equilibrium between good and evil. We are given the freedom to choose.

The Bible says:

> Do not even swear by your head, because you cannot make a single hair white or black. Just say "Yes" or "No"—anything else you say comes from the Evil One. (Matthew 5:36-37)

I believe this means that we must be able to clearly distinguish between good and evil. If we make a good decision, good spirits will go into motion, and doing good will feel good. If we choose evil, a bad spirit will begin to move, and the desire to do even more evil will give us pleasure.

Swedenborg's thinking was that all of our good acts were actually the acts of good spirits, and it was the spirits who made us want to do it.

The Law of the Guardian Angel

Each human spirit is accompanied by four spirits. Two are guardian angels: one to give us love the other to give us wisdom. And two spirits from Hell: one for evil, the other for falsehoods.

Humans are free to move among these four, and our soul matures as we learn to make decisions concerning our movements and behavior. Guardian angels are similar to the guardian spirits in Japanese culture. Their job is to keep the individual from becoming extremely bad and to make sure the intentions of good spirits coming from the Spiritual World are not obstructed. In a word, guardian angels protect us.

It is impossible for us humans to experience the movement of our guardian angels. This is to protect the notion of our free will.

The Law of the Appearance of Self

This teaching explains why humans are certain they think and act on their own volition, even though it is merely the outward appearance of such. It is similar to the relationship between the idea of the Earth as the center of the solar system and the truth of the Earth revolving around the sun. You may think the Earth stands still because you believe the sun revolves around it, but if you change your point of view, you can imagine that the Earth is actually the one in motion. This notion of appearance and actuality is a major part of the teachings of Swedenborg.

I noted that life is a reaction to some sort of action, an action that creates life. It's the same with the thoughts and actions of humans. Something from outside sets us to thinking. It is the power that gives us life. The source of this power is the creator of the universe. The creator will always try to mediate with the conscience of humans and set us on the right path, but the creator doesn't decide everything we think and do. That would rob us of free will, and we would have no reason to live. It is important to understand that the creator lets humans think and act on our own. With this, we are given the joy of life.

CHAPTER
FOUR

What Lives Inside You

As discussed, humans are like soil that receives the wisdom and love of God. Inflow from the fourth dimension, the Spiritual World, includes evil emotion from Hell as well as the love sent by God.

If, for example, you get an overwhelming desire to slug someone, Swedenborg says the feeling does not come from inside you. It is blown from Hell by an evil spirit. You may believe violent emotion wells up from inside, but it is actually from an evil spirit that has moved in on you.

We in the world of humans receive auras that come from our various experiences in life. Spirits coming to us from the Spiritual World choose human auras similar to their own. You see, even though they all live in the Spiritual World, spirits don't all operate at the same level. If a certain human aura matches a spirit very close to entering Heaven, it will serve as a guardian angel and aid the person in his or her growth. If, though, an aura matches a spirit in Hell, one bad thing after another will be sent that person's way!

In other words, it is not as if we humans have no responsibility for our bad thoughts. By adopting decadent values we invite evil spirits whose auras match ours.

Be careful of mediums and fortunetelling. The Bible writes that both of these should be avoided because they put us at risk of calling on evil spirits who will then latch onto us. It is extremely dangerous for humans to come into direct contact with such spirits. If anything goes wrong, one could become a slave to them.

The point is that even though we tend to believe we are acting alone, whether what we do is good or evil, all our actions are influenced by spirits. The Law of the Appearance of Self tells us that humans are given the appearance of acting on their own, but, just as the sun gives energy to plants, our energy does not come from a human source. It comes from Heaven. Heaven sends it via the Spiritual World, and spirits deliver it to us. Hell is also helpless without energy from Heaven. Inhabitants of Hell take the energy that comes from God to them and change it into bad energy, the polar opposite of its origin.

This makes it sound as though all of the world's problems are caused by spirits, and humans are no more than puppets operated by them. It also seems contradictory to the notion that God gave humans free will.

But as humans who are given life by Heaven, we receive energy for our souls from God, via spirits in the Spiritual World. Without spirits, our lifeline would be cut off. All plants get energy to grow from the sun. Why don't we consider the matter like this: we become ourselves, complete with a rich, open-minded value system based on the knowledge and experiences we acquire. Our auras, which are based on this process, are linked to spirits with similar auras. Good spirits bring with them good energy, and we use it to act in a good way. It's sort of like turning on the TV and learning to adjust the channels. Low-frequency ranges are Hell, and high-frequency ranges are Heaven. It is for us as individuals to decide which level of frequency we will adjust ourselves to.

Earlier, I explained that humans are receptacles of God's wisdom and love. We can also think of ourselves as receptacles of auras. Humans don't emit auras, we receive them. Each of our individual receptacles is adjusted to the level of our love. If it is noble, so will be the spirits we receive.

This means that even if God sends high-frequency levels of wisdom and love, if our receptacles are not tuned to receive them, we will miss them altogether, and instead catch the low-level frequencies of Hell and use them to fulfill greedy desires. God gives tacit approval to this sort of thing, because he created humans with free will.

So what do we learn from this? For humans to be saved in the true sense of the word, we have to banish evil spirits—all of the evil within us. We must strive to adjust our frequencies upward.

Again, it is the power of the spirits behind us that allow us to do good. The main freedom we have is the ability to adjust our levels of frequency. I interpret this to be the true meaning of free will for humans. The true job of humans during their lifetimes, our purpose for existing, is to raise the level of our frequencies to bring us closer to good.

Auras, good and bad

In recent years, vicious crimes have been on the upswing. And it seems to me that more and more people today have twisted personalities. According to the Law of the Guardian Angel, personalities can be influenced by spirits, which can easily latch on to people with decadent or unformed egos. Children, before their egos are fully formed, are usually strictly led by angels—who are good spirits. The best-case scenario is for a personality to be built on the foundation of an angel-led life, but if children are subject to parental abuse or lack of parental love, angels can lose control.

This makes it easy for a bad spirit to slip in and take over during the personality-building years. This is why the early years of childrearing are so important. Unless children get a sufficient amount of love from their parents, brain cells that are used to form personalities fail to grow properly.

Nobody is born evil or born to be a criminal. Human beings are nothing more than receptacles that are vulnerable to bad spirits. If subject to extremely bad influences, guardian angels lose their grip on a child. So you've got to pity the child who is taken over by a bad spirit. Saving a child from this takes a great amount of affectionate power from those around him or her.

Interestingly enough, greedy people seem to flock together. And considerate people seem to surround themselves with those of a similar nature. People who only complain tend to have friends who also have lots to spout off about.

You can say the same about spirits and humans. If a spirit gives a person a desire to become rich and the person embraces that desire, other spirits with similar auras will begin to gather round, and the avarice will grow even stronger.

It turns out that people who want money are never satisfied with how much they have. They may start out to earn $100 million, but once they get it—they want $200 million. And so on. If you imagine a single bad spirit calling another, and then another and another, I'm sure you'll understand why this sort of greed merely grows.

There are exceptions, though. If you only want money for yourself, you'll gain a flock of bad spirits. If you think of money as a way to help society and people you know who need it, though, you will be guided by good spirits. If God deems it necessary, you'll find the money you need.

To summarize, once a soul heads in the wrong direction, it is no simple task to redirect it. In order to create the kingdom of God inside you, you'll have to get rid of your bad aura and acquire a good one in its place. It won't be easy, but if you gain the knowledge you need and improve your value system, you can create an atmosphere receptive to good spirits and a new aura. Once that is done, good spirits will come flocking in. And good fortune will come your way. Both good and bad fortune are carried in by the spirits you have gathered, and that is why the word "fortune" is used.

So what exactly are the spirits that come to us? If you think in terms of similar wavelengths and values, the spirits of one's ancestors will most likely find it easiest to approach you because of your shared genetics.

Spirits live in the fourth dimension, but they originate in the three-dimensional world, so it is not surprising that they would share cultures and values. According to Swedenborg's teachings, there are heavens and hells for different nationalities. Similar values and concepts probably mean their auras tend to match.

Come out of the shadows

Among those who talk about spirits, there are many who speak of previous lives, citing their good or bad behavior in past lives, or their ancestors' lives, as reasons for particular abilities or wealth. But Christ never talked of such a thing. And I find Christ's teaching more logical. We are helpless if we believe our course is determined at birth by flaws in our previous lives. It is much more energizing to view life as an opportunity to make up for any discrepancies with which we were born.

What we receive from our ancestors in the form of DNA is no more than a provisional self on which to build. If you consider this "shadow" self to be your true self, you'll end up proud of your natural aptitudes and talents. Or, if you are not born gifted, you may drown in self-hatred. I believe life is our opportunity to build our true self out of our shadow self.

On the other hand, if you were blessed with a good background at birth, you might go through life without ever questioning a thing. It is when we confront negative aspects of ourselves that we are forced to struggle, when we first begin to wonder what is important in life. This can trigger us to seek the truth—and that is the intention of our creator.

Success in this life is not important to the creator. He wants humans to find truth and obtain eternal life. The Bible says the truth will give us a set of new clothes, and this certainly refers to being born again in the original sense. Many think of being "reborn" as coming back after death in another form, but that is not what it means at all.

To be born wealthy or talented is no real advantage in terms of creating your true self out of your shadow self. Such people tend to be satisfied with what they have and disinclined to change. That's why Christ said, "It is much harder for a rich person to enter the Kingdom of God than for a camel to go through the eye of a needle" (Luke 18:25).

This is the danger of mistaking your shadow self as your true self. The latter requires a lifetime of effort. We must seek our true selves by pursuing truth, wisdom and reason.

The difference between happiness and misery

In the Bible (Matthew 5:4), Christ's Sermon on the Mount tells us: "Happy are those who mourn; God will comfort them!"

The Bible often uses this sort of paradox to relay great truths. God gave humans many different forms of affection. Love that leads to mourning is no misfortune. It allows you to be comforted by God.

Think about it this way. What if it were your child who was mourning? Wouldn't you want to give him or her something greater to replace that sadness? God has a similar relationship with humanity. God is greater than us and so in a position to comfort us with something wonderful when we mourn. We're dealing with God here, so we cannot imagine what it will be. It might be something everlasting that transcends all different dimensions. The love of God will always appear after a human has experienced pain or sadness. We go through these difficult experiences because we do not know the truth. Under the light of truth, our pain will grow into comfort and joy.

A feeling of happiness is the emotion of joy. There is no one who does not prefer to be happy; it is one of the most basic of human needs. What then *is* happiness?

You might think that happiness is an objective human act, but you would be wrong. Some sort of external stimulus is necessary. Happiness is one reaction to external events. Some external stimuli generate in us emotions of anger or sadness; some generate happiness. But without some form of stimulus, it is impossible to feel joy. And once we have felt joy, we want to feel it again.

Neurology has demonstrated that we make unconscious value judgments as to how any event affects us. When our brains decide that something is pleasurable, we feel it has value for us. But when the brain decides something is disagreeable, we tend to consider it worthless.

Pleasure judgments are made in the amygdala, a part of the brain inside the temporal lobes. When the amygdala goes to work, the temporal lobes spread a feeling of joy throughout our body. This is the mechanism of good feelings, the way happiness works.

How, then, does your brain decide if something is a pleasure? It first compares the sensory input with the desires of your heart. With repetition, this process becomes reflexive. Once an experience is registered as pleasurable, it becomes something we think of as good.

Once something is registered as good or bad, it becomes a part of our lives and reactions to it are not easily changed. This is because a certain law of inertia is at work in the human heart. After a direction has been set, it takes a great deal of power to change or shift it. For better or for worse, we need this inertia. Without it, our personalities would be unstable—we might be full of charity one day, and scary and intimidating the next. We would be very hard to get along with. In the same way, it is not easy to revise our view of something proven to provide pleasure. This is what makes a profound switch in values—a paradigm shift—so difficult to achieve.

Unfortunately, we humans often fail to find pleasure in things we should be able to judge as truthful, and instead find them disagreeable. For example, we tend to take pleasure in the ephemeral thrill of getting ahead of others—being promoted more quickly or doing better in school. Sharing is less fun than winning something for ourselves. This sort of convoluted value system is proof that this is an age where Heaven and Earth are upside down.

This backward view, egotistical evil, has been imprinted in our genes and passed from one generation to the next. As a value system it has become so ingrained in humankind that it would take an incredible force to change it even slightly. Even if we have a vague feeling that something is wrong, we need a great deal of energy to make any changes.

Our ancestors found pleasure over and over again in egotistical evil. Even when they recognized the truth, they ignored it to avoid forgoing pleasure. They refused to accept the pain of truth. It would become a cross for them to bear.

Al Gore, the former US vice-president and Nobel Peace Prize winner, described looming environmental problems as "an inconvenient truth." To me, that perfectly describes the difficulty of making a paradigm shift. For those attached to conventional notions of pleasure, celestine truth is certainly "inconvenient." But until we come change our notions of pleasure and success, we will not be able to set the universe right and restore Heaven and Earth to their proper positions.

Interestingly enough, we all have chances to do so. One opportunity is paying attention to qualms of conscience. For example, someone who makes a living scamming others out of their hard-earned money may wonder at times if this is really a good way to make a living. This pang of conscience is a visit from Heaven, proof of an inflow of divine wisdom. If the person receiving it recognizes it and changes in response, inflow from Heaven will increase greatly. And that person will begin to evolve as a human living in truth. If such a person can be patient enough to listen to his or her conscience and make efforts to live in truth, guardian angels will quickly get to work. Gradually notions of pleasure and displeasure will change, and a soul will be reborn into eternal happiness.

Who decides what makes you happy?

When our brains decide that something is pleasurable, the decision is made in reference to a value system. And each of us has our own version; no two are exactly the same. Our values differ because our experiences and the knowledge we gain are different. Some people derive happiness from doing good, others enjoy doing bad. What we tend to have in common, though, is values rooted in self-interest—achieving some sort of benefit.

Other value decisions are innate, either physically or temperamentally. Some get a great deal of pleasure from music that leaves others unmoved. Adventurers are thrilled by new challenges, and generally dislike authority.

Mostly, though, our values are shaped by the environments in which we are brought up, genes we inherit from our parents, as well as their value systems and social backgrounds.

Thus, a child born into a family of doctors may be expected to go to medical school. And following in the family footsteps would probably make such a child happy. Personally, I think there are lots of interesting occupations to consider, but for that particular child, failure to become a doctor might result in a degree of desperation we could only imagine.

In other words, to someone raised in an environment where the standard of success is to become a doctor, anything else represents failure. But accepting that standard is an individual decision.

While beetle larvae are considered delicacies in some countries, most Japanese would find them revolting, just as people from elsewhere disdain the fermented soybeans we love in Japan.

There are many aspects of our values that we set for ourselves, but with strong influence from our surroundings. This is a key point in considering the meaning of true happiness. What we think of as happiness is usually influenced by what society around us tells us is happiness, and by the attitudes of parents and friends. In this way we pursue preconceived notions of happiness.

We are brainwashed by our day and age

Your personal value system is at the root of all the decisions you make in life. And your value system is molded by the environment and social background in which you grew up. A child whose parents admonish him to "hit back twice as hard" will incorporate that into his or her value system without a second thought. If you see the large homes of rich people on TV and are told over and over that this represents success, you'll believe it. In this day and age when educational background is given the highest value, graduating from a so-called good school, advancing in one's career and rising to a position of prominence are seen as hallmarks of success.

These environmental influences become imprinted in our brains alongside genetic traits inherited from our ancestors. Once all these influences are established inside us, they are almost impossible to overwrite. It takes a lot of work to turn a value system on its head.

You could almost call the entire process brainwashing. The value system of a certain society in a certain age becomes fixed inside the brain of the individual. I call this "brainwashing of our day and age." It happens in all cultures during all ages.

Before World War II, it was a common dream among Japanese boys to join the army and become a general. That was certainly a form of social brainwashing. Nowadays, people want money and a position with a high social status. This is modern brainwashing.

We should be aware that value systems adopted from the social environment are extremely subjective, and that they change over the years. There aren't many boys in Japan today who dream of becoming generals. In decades to come, there may be nobody left who wants to make money or climb the corporate ladder.

For this very reason, it is vital that, before you go out looking for happiness, you reflect on your own notions of success, the goals you want to set and the desires you'd like to realize. You need to thoroughly reevaluate your own value system.

If you find it impossible to become happy, your values might have you at the wrong starting point. Inside yourself you have all you need to be either happy or miserable.

Joy of heaven, joy of earth

Our inclination to compete is the biggest obstacle in the pursuit of human happiness. In the world we live in, competition is what keeps academics, work, and sports alive. And there is no question that paying more to winners is one of the key mechanisms of growth. But since any personal satisfaction we get from competition comes from within and not from God, I call it "worldly joy."

Sure, winning brings happiness, but that is only fleeting. Once you win, you want to do it over and over again, and you may even develop a fear of losing. I believe that we have reached a point in our existence where we should question whether winning a competition can bring true happiness. It seems to me that society based on competition has reached its limits. The race among countries and corporations to grab non-renewable resources has brought our natural environment to the brink of destruction.

It is true that competition can have good results. Humans need the spur of it to get down to work. You might even call it a necessary evil, but we should understand that it is an evil that serves a purpose in achieving goals. Competition for its own sake should be avoided. Ignoring this fact and merely competing to win in a never-ending repetition of happiness and anxiety merely fills one with fleeting worldly joy. It is like an addiction to shopping—no matter how much you buy, you still want more. Competition can be just as addictive and just as unfulfilling.

Though the "evil joy" of competition is an ephemeral one, there are joys in this world that continue on and on. There is the joy of keeping God's creations from extinction, and the joy of living in peace together. I call these "heavenly joys."

Worker bees spend their lives in support of the queen bee, and they do whatever is necessary to protect her and the hive.

To the human eye, the queen's subjects all sacrifice themselves for her, but that it is not the way it is at all. These creatures merely place their priority on the continuation and flourishing of their species.

In the days when Heaven and Earth were connected, all of humanity must have felt joy in keeping themselves and each other alive. Humans have those genes, too—we are programmed to feel heavenly joy. Now, however, when Heaven and Earth are turned upside down, we all aim to be the queen bee, and we compete to get there.

The goal of God, the creator of all life, is for all of God's creatures to live together in happiness. With this in mind, shouldn't our greatest heavenly joy be to serve? "To serve" means to support our neighbor, become seeds, make new flowers bloom, and aim for the eternal continuation of the human race. This doesn't mean, of course, that we must suppress our individuality or forsake our own interests. There is great beauty in the distinctiveness of individuality, and the variety of flowers that could bloom would only add to the beauty of the world.

If all of humanity found joy in supporting and serving each other, and if it was their goal in life, what a wonderful place our society would be. The joy would not be one of self-satisfaction, but one of awe from deep inside our souls. Our souls are programmed to feel this sort of strong emotion.

And, as it turns out, the joy of serving evokes a much more powerful feeling of joy and emotion than does self-centered worldly joy. Why? Because worldly joy is not something that can be shared—it is distinctly personal. The joy of serving, on the other hand, can spread to all people, spreading its aura farther and farther, and resulting in a wave of joyous synergy.

Unfortunately, modern humanity has never experienced such joy. God is waiting for human beings to repent, change and expand their focus, and enter into a state of heavenly joy. The ultimate joy would be the universe in a state of coexistence and co-prosperity.

The Bible says that the greatest joy of angels, servants of God, will come when the human race repents and they are all linked together.

> Or suppose a woman who has ten silver coins loses one of them—what does she do? She lights a lamp, sweeps her house, and looks carefully everywhere until she finds it. When she finds it, she calls her friends and neighbors together, and says to them, "I am so happy I found the coin I lost. Let us celebrate!" In the same way, I tell you, the angels of God rejoice over one sinner who repents. (Luke 15:8-10)

The angels in Heaven all await the day when humans repent from the depths of their hearts.

Nurturing the kingdom within

While many people believe that they form their own view of the world and their own set of values, as I've shown, our views and values are actually shaped by our genetic inheritance and brainwashing by our contemporary environment.

If someone born into wealth gets his or her first taste of economic hardship as an adult, it tends to come as quite a shock—where someone born into poverty would take it in stride.

If, however, that rich person has a broad outlook, if he or she understands there are many different value systems in the world, such a person can probably ride out a rough patch without too much stress. A broad perspective keeps the heart healthy no matter what values the age or culture tries to force on you.

Our bodies are nourished and grow when we eat food, and our hearts and souls grow when we are exposed to a broad range of knowledge and experience. This helps us develop a strong sense of values. One thing we tend to forget, though, is that our hearts and souls do not grow automatically with the passage of years. False information can lead to mistaken values. We also need to be sure the knowledge we obtain is true.

While our physical bodies give us unmistakable signs of malnutrition, our hearts do not. We have to take good care of our hearts, noting any lack of nutrition or stunted growth. True knowledge is the nutrition for which the heart hungers. By the same token, absorbing bad knowledge will lead to improper values that damage those around us.

As children lack knowledge and experience, the kingdom in their hearts has yet to develop. Children are happy just to play hide-and-seek, thinking only of their own needs. Adults today have a great deal of knowledge and experience, which means we should have everything we need for a noble kingdom in our hearts. We are also able to comprehend high levels of joy. But when fed on bad knowledge the hearts of adults are capable of evil far beyond a child's imagination.

The kingdom of the heart is each individual's conscience. And where our physical shapes, our height and weight, are limited, there is no limit to the world of our conscience. By gaining a large amount of true knowledge, our conscience can stretch to a limitless extent, and it can be changed.

What's more, our conscience can be expanded to transcend this world and move into higher dimensions. There are limits to the conscience of those who see only the world around them, but those who can move higher into the fourth and fifth dimensions will have a richness of spirit that few can imagine.

Don't limit yourself to this world—look to Heaven

The other day, a bank customer brought along an interesting book. His father, a man of strong religious faith, had written his memoirs with the title, *A Fool*. I thought it was a great title.

None of us want to admit how foolish we are. We want others to see us as exceptional, somehow set apart from the rest of humanity. But no matter how much good we do, no matter how big the company we build, our efforts are insignificant in the context of the entire universe.

What, then, is a worthwhile activity to pursue? I believe it is to spend one's life in search of truth and a righteous system of values. When we go to the spiritual world, our accomplishments in this world will mean little. We'll have no need to wear beautiful clothes or otherwise adorn ourselves. All that remains when our vanity has been stripped away is our sense of reason and our values. If we want to polish them before we go, we need to stand before Heaven and reflect on ourselves. If we have failed to learn any heavenly truths, we must recognize that there is no good in our own egos, and that we are nothing but self-centered fools. The Bible says:

> Sell all your belongings and give the money to the poor. Provide for yourselves purses that don't wear out, and save your riches in Heaven, where they will never

> decrease, because no thief can get to them, and no moth can destroy them. (Luke 12:23)

"Belongings" here means everything you are proud of—riches and honor, status, and other accomplishments. "Riches in Heaven" will be the truth and love you have built up inside you on Earth. These are what you take with you into eternal life.

While you are on Earth, the outside kingdom, your physical appearance is inherited from your parents, so there is not much you can do about that. But you can buy all the clothes you want as long as you have the money. According to Swedenborg's teachings, our clothes in Heaven will be given to us by God, depending on how much truth we obtained while on Earth. Those who obtained the truth of God are dressed in radiant garments. People who have no truth are dressed in dirty rags.

In addition, people who receive the love of God have a beautiful appearance (soul), while those who are strongly self-centered and full of malice have the features of beasts and monsters.

No matter how much status we have on this Earth, no matter how much wealth or beauty we have, none of it will do us any good when we go to Heaven unless we have prepared an inner kingdom of truth and love.

John the Baptist baptized those who repented their sins. As a predecessor of Christ, he preached that "no one can have anything unless God gives it" (John 3:27). He instructed us to give up the treasures of this world and receive truth and love from Heaven.

Only when we humbly accept that we are "fools unless we are accepted by God" will the egotistical power that prevents the connection between Heaven and Earth weaken, and will God shower us with warmth and light. Plants in nature grow and grow when they have the warmth and light of the sun. In the same way, humans will grow and bloom just like beautiful flowers. Only then will we realize the limitations of our physical selves and recognize the presence of God, creator of the universe. That is when our souls will begin to grow.

Standards of good and evil

Few would disagree that taking the life of another human is a sin. But would it be a sin to kill an evil and genocidal dictator? Not many would think so.

In peacetime, anyone who killed dozens of young people would be held responsible for a heinous crime. But in wartime someone who obliterates enemy troops is considered a hero. Some would say that war is an absolute evil. But if you are attacked, what can you reasonably do to defend yourself?

This is the sort of conundrum that convinces me that notions of sin in the real world are alarmingly relative.

Since many things are accepted by some cultures and condemned by others, are there any universal standards by which to make ultimate decisions? The only thing I can think of is the intention of the creator, which I believe is peaceful cohabitation and the continuity of life.

We can compare the universe as a life form to the sixty trillion cells that make up the human body. The cells form each organ; the heart and lungs, and so on. Together they form a body in which each piece is independent, but all work toward the common goal of maintaining life.

Each cell has to work in harmony with the others. If each began to pursue its own initiative, the body would quickly become dysfunctional. In the same way, we humans must work together to keep the universe and the Earth alive. It is why we maintain organic relationships with each other. Cells "do good" by maintaining the life form to which they belong. Anything in opposition to that objective is wrong. It is the same for humans, creations of God. We do "good" when we work toward the continuation of the universe, the Earth, and humanity. So it is reasonable to assume that anything contrary to that is wrong, or evil. When we think in terms of our creator, universal standards of good and evil are really very simple.

There is, however, a difference between humans and cells in that God gave humans free will. If we were all forced to conform, it would be totalitarianism, and we would no longer be human.

We are free to eat the foods we like. But if we abuse our freedom and consume to excess, we damage our health. But when we harm ourselves at least we have pain as an alarm signal.

In the same way, although our creator respects our freedom, when we become a threat to the existence of the universe or humankind, there is always some kind of alarm that alerts us to the presence of evil in order to protect the principle of coexistence. This alarm could come from nature, which has the ability to protect and heal itself. You might call it a form of risk management. The universe has natural healing powers that lead evil into good, and it might even be that this power is constantly attempting to lead humans toward good.

> If people hear my message and do not obey it, I will not judge them. I came, not to judge the world, but to save it. Those who reject me and do not accept my message have one who will judge them. The words I have spoken will be their judge on the last day! (John 12:47-48)

In our minds, a natural catastrophe may feel like divine punishment, but a piece of steel forced to bend will spring back into its original shape. This power to repair and recreate is the natural healing power of the universe. Christ said that the truth will save us. Even if humans refuse to live according to God's words of truth, those words have the power to spring back and propel humans back toward them. It is how truth protects the life form of the universe.

CHAPTER FIVE

The Proper Use of Love

To live life in harmony, without wars or other struggles, is for most people an ideal existence. If we all want it so much, then what prevents us from achieving peaceful coexistence? I believe it is our selfish egos, our love for this world, and our craving for power. Each of these is a form of love, and we all have some of each of them within us, but they do not represent the love God has in mind for us. In fact they are exactly the opposite.

A person with a strong ego is filled with the need for recognition. A strong ego is prone to hatred and desire for revenge when thwarted. At worst, it leads to murderous anger. Another sign of a need for glory is the joy of winning in competition. Christ taught us this:

> Make certain you do not perform your religious duties in public so that people will see what you do. If you do

these things publicly, you will not have any reward from your Father in Heaven.

So when you give something to a needy person, do not make a big show of it, as the hypocrites do in the houses of worship and on the streets. They do it so that people will praise them. I assure you, they have already been paid in full. (Matthew 6:1-2)

and

But how terrible for you who are rich now; you have had your easy life!

How terrible for you who are full now; you will go hungry!

How terrible for you who laugh now; you will mourn and weep!

How terrible when all people speak well of you; their ancestors said the very same things about the false prophets." (Luke 6:24-26)

In these passages Christ speaks to our raw needs for recognition and praise.

There are very few who wouldn't appreciate praise and recognition for their good deeds. Praise might even encourage us to do more good in its pursuit. Unfortunately, though, we tend to lose sight of our original intentions. Do we want to do good for its own sake, or is it praise we crave? It is an easy trap to fall into, and getting out of it is not a simple matter. Our ego is always there, somewhere in the depths of our hearts, getting us in trouble.

I don't think it's a bad thing for someone who has made some money in business to start up a charity, say, to protect the environment. On the contrary, it is laudable. But even philanthropic activities should be examined to make sure the doers are treating the people closest to them (i.e., the company that made the money in the first place) well before they take off to do further "good."

How are family and employees treated? Are suppliers paid and customers satisfied? If families are left to fend for themselves and the company is left in chaos while the boss runs around doing "good deeds," the situation ought to be reevaluated. It doesn't matter how much good someone is doing for society as a whole. Anyone who is unable to care for his or her own family has no business dashing off to faraway lands to help others. I have even heard of cases where employee salaries were cut to leave more money for the CEO's pet projects.

Ego, love of this world, and love of power are a few sins that are in opposition to the principle of coexistence. They are the source of evil and a joy to Hell. We all have a little bit of each of these sins, but we must acknowledge them as bottomless pits, a thirst that can never be slaked, a hunger that grows no matter how much they are fed. They are like cancer cells reproducing at the cost of the life that feeds them. History is strewn with those who became slaves to these three sins and drowned in the pain and despair to which they led.

God is the source of love that gives life to others. In the early days of humanity, people were filled with awe of this love and were able to live in unity. Gradually, though, humans blessed with freedom were drawn to more sensual joys and began to rebel against the divine call for coexistence. This was the beginning of the fall of humankind. As people were diverted by the notion that sensual joy was truth, they gave themselves over to the three evil loves.

We are all susceptible to ego, love of this world, and love of power because we have inherited them from our ancestors in the form of instinct. They are the story of Adam and Eve.

God told Adam and Eve that they could eat from any tree in the Garden of Eden, but they must not eat from the Tree of Knowledge of Good and Evil. But Adam and Eve were tempted by sensual joys, as symbolized by the snake, and disobeyed God's command. The Tree of Knowledge of Good and Evil symbolizes the values of the "false world."

This is not to say it is a sin to think about good and evil or to know about truth. The point is to have the correct objectives and priorities. When people ignore love and look for truth, each will arrive at a different notion of truth, and this leads to conflict and war. Thus murder and war are the products of individuals who insist on their own personal version of truth. Anyone who holds love as his or her top priority will recoil from murder and war. No matter what the ideology, when love is the top priority, differing parties will search for the key to coexistence.

Even in church, where faith and love are much discussed, love often remains secondary to faith. The emphasis is on following specific beliefs in order to achieve salvation. Somewhere along the way love is lost, and people are torn apart by differences in faith.

Know yourself

How, then, can we control ego, love of this world, and love of power? Even though we know better humans are unable to change. It all comes down to understanding that humanity is basically evil. We must believe that our ancestors rebelled against the joy of Heaven and found delight in their own prosperity, and that this is what drives our own instincts. We need to understand that the evil within us must be controlled, and we can do this by becoming humble and doing our best to avoid what is bad. Then gradually, we can release ourselves from our base desires.

You've got to be careful, though, of the word "humble." Once someone said to me, "You might be considered humble if you never put on airs and always deferred to others. But what if you are doing it so others will admire your humility?"

This is a good point. What this person has described is not humility. It is no more than the pretence of humility.

Someone else made a similar comment: "Humility means making a show of holding yourself in low esteem, but it ends up looking exactly like pride."

The Japanese word for "humble" does have such nuances, and it is often used to mean "wordlessly accepting the opinions of others" and "deferring to authority no matter what you actually think." But true humility does not mean sacrificing your own opinion or perpetually suffering in silence. This is not humility—it is remaining silent to suit one's own purposes.

A truly humble person reacts instinctively to curb the joy of evil inside himself or herself. By recognizing our capacity for pride if given position and authority, or even when flattered, we are able to exercise self-control that keeps us from becoming proud and arrogant. Humility is something we get when we fully understand that not being humble will mean our own downfall; it recognizes the evil inside ourselves.

John, Christ's beloved disciple, wrote the following in a letter: "If we say that we have no sin, we deceive ourselves, and there is no truth in us." (1 John 1:8)

It is difficult for most people to see their own evil. Humility begins only when we see that there is nothing more to us than our egos. And egos are basically bad because they oppose the universal principle of coexistence. Egos hurt the people around us and they lead to conflict.

The English word "humble" has the same root as "human." In other words, to be humble is to be human. And, as I mentioned, the root of "human" is *hum*, or "soil."

Soil is not itself a life form, but it carries and nurtures life within it. Humans, like dirt, are given life from an outside force. The source of the word "human" is based on the idea that we have a soul, or conscience, only after life is blown into us from outside. Once we understand that we are nothing unless Heaven decides to give us life, then we become human-like, or "humble."

Pride is better than hypocrisy

Hypocrisy is often confused with humility. We all know it is important to say "thank you." I've heard that there are even books that teach that constant repetition of the words "thank you," whether or not you really mean them, will bring you good fortune. No one will argue that being thankful is a bad thing. But I believe that you may be setting yourself up for disappointment if you think everything will go well as long as you repeat the same words over and over. In fact, you would be reciting some simple words that meant nothing to you, all in the expectation of profit.

You might even be feigning humility in order to gain wealth or recognition. This is hypocrisy rather than humility. In my opinion, it's much better to come right out and be arrogant if that is the way you really feel.

If you live a life of pride and arrogance, sooner or later the rest of the world will penalize you for it, and this means you will have an opportunity to change your ways. Hypocrites tend to be revered in a strange sort of way, and they thus have fewer opportunities to realize what they are doing wrong.

Mother Teresa is a fine example of someone who knew her own weaknesses. It is amazing that such a great person could have had a fear of her own pride. It is said that she always said her prayers in a corner of the church where she wouldn't be noticed. She knew very well that a truly humble person is the most vulnerable to pride and hypocrisy. Being humble means paying close attention to one's own weaknesses.

Sin and vocation: Human DNA

That humans are inherently sinful is one of the basic teachings of Christ. But sin is not necessarily the sort of things you may imagine—such as violence or stealing. Such crimes result from sin, but are not necessarily the sins themselves. Nor is there anything morally wrong in the fact that we are born to err. The original human sin was to resist and reject the principles of coexistence. It means living to please one's own desires rather than finding joy in giving life to others. Thus the worst of sinners love only themselves. It leads to an effect similar to cancer cells.

The Buddhist word for sin is "karma." The two words are not exactly the same, but I think we can use them interchangeably here.

When a plant puts out a bud, and then a branch which sprouts leaves, flowers and, finally, fruit, it is all part of the plan written in the DNA of the seed. We can use this to imagine humans in the process of becoming children of God.

Three levels of genes determine the growth of our psyche. They appear one at a time, the first during childhood, then adolescence and, finally, in adulthood. You can think of this process in terms of the evolution of the human race in ancient, modern, and future times.

The first level of human DNA is innocence. Angels protect children throughout their childhood. A baby's smile recalls the simple hearts of ancient humans who lived in the age of innocent love.

The second level of DNA holds the ego. These are genes full of built-up selfish desire passed down from our ancestors.

And no matter how good we may think we are, we all have some of it. This DNA first appears during adolescence, and it brings on the ego, with a period of rebelliousness in its wake. When comparing it to the history of humankind, it is easy to see that we are in an age where the ego is given full play.

The third type of DNA gives humans purity of wisdom. When childish innocence gives way to evil desires, our egos are strong. Finally, though, a love of wisdom is established, and we can become children of God. Humans must first of all recognize our inherent evil to bring out reason and conscience that can reject it. When we can win out over evil, the purity we receive from God grows into purity of wisdom. It appears as an intuitive ability to control human desire. With conscience and reason, we are born again, and we can become merciful, in the same way God is.

The Bible describes it like this:

> No! Love your enemies and do good to them; lend and expect nothing back. You will then have a great reward, and you will be children of the Most High God; for He is good to the ungrateful and the wicked. Be merciful just as your Father is merciful. (Luke 6:35-36)

This third type of DNA does not appear until adulthood. In fact, some people end their lives without ever being able to make use of it. It is my fervent hope that, in the future, people will be able to achieve an age full of love for their fellow humans based on a manifestation of this DNA.

The key point here is making one's way through childhood and the rebellious period, which symbolizes evil, and reaching the age when the DNA of pure wisdom can bloom. After all, cherry trees flower because they make it through the cold of winter.

This is consistent with the Buddhist notion that an evil person is the best object of salvation. A sinner knows more than anyone about evil. If such a person repents and changes heart, it will be based on full knowledge of the power of evil, and it will lead to a truly tranquil spirit.

Self-hatred is an opportunity for an awakening

The Bible says, "Happy are those who know they are spiritually poor; the Kingdom of Heaven belongs to them!" (Matthew 5:3).

You might wonder why it is so fortunate to be spiritually poor. But these paradoxical words are a hint at the DNA process described above.

Take, for example, a child born to virtuous parents. If he or she grows up in the parents' footsteps, it won't be much of a feat; the child has simply imitated the people who raised him or her. The slightest temptation might easily lead such a child down an evil path.

On the other hand, let's say we have a child of criminals, born and raised in a bad environment. What if this child grew up to be virtuous? The reason and conscience such a child would require to overcome evil would be strong and steadfast.

In either case, the most important point would be for both children to see the evil in themselves. In natural disaster or war, we are often exposed to unbearable human evil. In the aftermath of earthquakes we often hear of looters who break into stores and homes and steal everything they can get their hands on. I don't mean to defend such behavior, but it makes sense when you realize that this is the true nature of humans.

Some people are filled with self-hatred because they see the evil within themselves. There is nothing unnatural about this either. It is important to appreciate that self-hatred comes from a deep-seated desire to be good. Self-hatred means that God has planted the seeds of conscience to give that person a chance to change his or her life.

Still, problems arise when such a person fails to realize what is happening, believing only that he or she is worthless. Despair can lead to suicide when life's prospects appear bleak. Truth is needed here; it is all it takes to live a full and powerful life.

A merciful heart is sent from Heaven

So why doesn't God quickly judge and punish us when we do wrong? You'd think that almighty God, creator of the universe, would avoid dealing with such bothersome creatures by making human beings good to start out with.

Again, it is helpful to think of antigens that start a disease and antibodies that fight them off. For the first six months of life a baby retains antibodies from its mother's womb, but after that the baby must generate its own antibodies to fight disease. In order to be immune to a pathogen, you must have a little bit of it in your system. Let's take tuberculosis. If you have the tubercular bacillus inside you, your body will produce an antibody to fight it. But if you have not had the disease you cannot generate the antibodies needed to overcome it. For this, you need to be vaccinated with a very weak version of the pathogen in order to develop immunity.

It's the same with evil. To build up the proper immunity, you've got to have it inside you. You must have the seeds of evil and sin within you in order to win out against it.

Where evil is concerned, the antibody comes from the human conscience. No matter how strong a vaccine, it won't work unless there is an immune system to accept it. The immune system is a good metaphor for the conscience. And the conscience is made from the knowledge of love that flows from God. The power of love is the only thing that can claim victory over the antigen of evil. When we get a deep sense of evil or sin, we feel strong pangs of conscience. What can we use to heal it? This is where we come into contact with the love of a merciful God. It is when the "merciful heart that can forgive" is manifest—right there in that third DNA, where it has been since the beginning of creation.

We have to realize that although God is always ready to intervene with merciful love, humans cannot accept it until the time is right. In other words, God gave humans free will knowing all along that we would choose evil. God watches as we fall into depravity, all the while waiting for us to recognize the evil within, the evil inherited from our ancestors. God waits for us to understand that evil is at the root of all misfortune and unhappiness—knowing that consideration and thankfulness will be born out of our struggle with evil.

In this way, we resemble Christ. Christ, the almighty God, was born as a human child into the limited world of the third dimension. He had within him a terrible disease, evil that he had to struggle with his entire life until he died on the cross.

Christ was born at a time when humans had given themselves completely to self-love. And he paid the price for our sins in order to create antigens that generate a love powerful enough to overcome evil.

His trials were like a terrible fever, one that generated the most powerful and merciful antibody known to humanity, one that meant life for even the worst of murderers, offering them resurrection from the dead. This antibody had the power of a merciful love so strong it could change even the worst sinner into a good person. The life, death and resurrection of Christ represent the greatest sacrifice that we humans are capable of understanding. When this antibody was made, we humans were once again linked to Heaven because of the wisdom of truth and love it offered us. Because of it we are capable of forgiveness, love, and receiving love from our neighbor.

First, avoid evil

I've been interested in science ever since I was a child. In my early teens, I collected butterflies. I nurtured the eggs at home and watched them hatch into larvae. I fed them until they made cocoons, and waited for them to emerge as butterflies. In later years, I began to think about how the butterfly evolves: caterpillar, cocoon, butterfly. You could apply it to the evolution of human beings.

Those of us living busily and noisily in the third dimension resemble caterpillars that creep along the Earth. We're so busy and focused on what we're doing that we forget about the sky spreading out endlessly above us. We are oblivious. So we satisfy ourselves fulfilling ephemeral desires: making money, attaining status, or indulging in vanity.

Then, one day, we may realize that we were born with evil inside of us, and that we have nothing unless we receive it from Heaven. If we get that far, we are in a cocoon, rendered immobile by the realization that all we have done has been a rejection of Heaven, and that from here on we will not be able to move without its power. When we are able to reject our evil selves, our third set of DNA will kick in and we will be reborn with a new soul. This stage can be symbolized as a butterfly coming out of its cocoon.

Anyone can turn into a butterfly, a lovely creature that flies anywhere it wants to go, pollinating flowers in its quest for honey. A metamorphosis very much like this is programmed into our DNA. Unfortunately, most people believe that there is nothing for them beyond the caterpillar stage. We go up and down, through good times and bad, experiencing pleasure and pain based on what is in front of us. It might be good to remember that none of that will mean much when we're flying unimpeded through the air, looking at caterpillars from above.

I don't know if my interest in the metamorphosis of butterflies was accidental or destined to happen. It just might be that my creator wanted me to spend time observing so that I would understand how important it is for us to undergo a similar change—a hint from my creator to get my soul on an evolutionary track.

An adult bird does its part to get its offspring safely into the world by keeping the eggs warm. The warmth of the bird is symbolic of human love. Humans are given life through love, and they will not grow unless they have wisdom tempered with love. Flowers do not bloom in the light of winter. It is the warm light of spring that makes that happen. Summer light is even hotter, and it is what farmers need for their crops.

We can learn from plants what humans need to grow and mature. As a seed, a plant has the capacity to put out a sprout. We can compare this to a human who has attained truth. The process by which the light and heat of the sun make plants grow is the same as accepting the truth and love of God. It is the process by which we grow spiritually. Plants follow a natural cycle. It's what keeps them growing properly. If flowers bloomed as soon as they sprouted, they would be unable to bear fruit, and the entire plant would be destroyed. In the same way, we cannot go against the evolutionary process. By following the evolution of the universe, our souls can mature.

Plants grow facing the sun; this is called heliotropism. This, too, affords us insight into ourselves. Turning toward the light and warmth of the sun, and away from darkness, is symbolic of turning away from evil and looking toward love and truth.

Our innate evil will often lead us to turn toward darkness, and we must struggle to avoid it. It may seem that avoiding evil is a passive action, and that doing good is active, but there is a trap in that reasoning. If, for example, you gave something to the poor and told no one, you could never say that it hadn't been personally satisfying to do it.

Sadly, it may be that no modern human being is capable of "doing good." All the "good" we think we do may be mere hypocrisy. If a person truly comprehends love, he or she might be able to do good because they know what selfless love is. But most humans would only be forcing themselves into hypocrisy. In that case, it is a much better idea to go back a step and first try to live a life without doing evil. By not doing evil, we can align ourselves with the evolution of the universe, ride those upward currents, and undergo steady spiritual growth. By avoiding evil, learning truth, and moving into the light of truth, we will eventually feel the warmth and joy of light.

Judge and be judged; forgive and be forgiven

In our daily lives, consciously or not, we judge the words and actions of others. A humble person understands how arrogant it is to judge someone else.

You may know this Bible passage:

> Do not judge others, so that God will not judge you, for God will judge you in the same way you judge others, and he will apply to you the same rules you apply to others.

Why, then, do you look at the speck in your brother's eye and pay no attention to the log in your own eye? How dare you say to your brother, "Please, let me take that speck out of your eye," when you have a log in your own eye? You hypocrite! First take the log out of your own eye, and then you will be able to see clearly to take the speck out of your brother's eye. (Matthew 7:1-5)

There are, for certain, people who willfully cause trouble. And our creator knew there would be such people on Earth when he gave us free will. God watches such behavior silently, and indeed, intends for it to be there. But in the end, only God can judge. Humans cannot judge others because we do not know the plans God has to complete our souls. If such behavior endangered the evolution of the universe, where we are all destined to coexist for eternity, God would certainly mete out some form of punishment to keep it under control. If God chooses not to control or punish a person, it is a sign that it is all a part of his plan.

Sometimes God leaves evil in place to serve as a bad example from which we can learn. God is teaching us and also has something in mind for the soul of the person causing a problem. When it comes down to it, when we come face to face with evil we shouldn't be quick to judge it, but instead consider whether we can learn from it.

There are lots of things about life that we find unfair. From the cosmic viewpoint, though, it is all part and parcel of the soul's journey to enlightenment. The Bible tells us there are things we, who have no idea of God's will, should never say, such as, "he is a failure as a human being" or "she is beyond saving." There is always a possibility that a person can suddenly repent and change, and spread love to others. Here is another Bible passage:

> If you forgive others the wrongs they have done to you, your Father in Heaven will also forgive you. But if you do not forgive others, then your Father will not forgive the wrongs you have done. (Matthew 6:14-15)

As long as human beings are equipped with the second DNA, we will always be tempted in an evil atmosphere. We are all at risk of sinning. You must never forget that you, too, are a weak person. Remember God's command to forgive others. A forgiving heart is one way of loving our neighbors that can give hope to modern society in its miserable condition.

No matter how bad a person is, while they live they have the possibility of being reborn, repenting their sins, and attaining a true spirit. If they fail to repent, however, they will become tragic souls destined to suffer in Hell. And getting out of Hell is not easy. God, of course, pities those souls and tries to save them. If they confess and repent their sins, they will move up to the Spiritual World. There they will remain "in training" until they are ready to ascend into Heaven. It might take millions of years for that to happen. To avoid this seemingly endless agony, it would be best for these souls to change their ways while still on Earth. The greatest form of neighborly love would be to gently prod them in that direction.

In any case, God works under the assumption that all humans are capable of repenting, and for that reason, we humans must not judge. The only thing we are allowed to do is forgive.

Unfortunately, forgiving is not always an easy thing to do. Indeed, we have our ancestors' DNA urging us to "give back as good as you get." It is this DNA that prevents us from forgiving, and instead makes us quick to judge. When we say, "I can never forgive this!" the emotion behind it is rooted in Hell. And as long as one has that, the poison in it will fill one with suffering and agony. This is a formidable piece of baggage to lug into the afterlife. So no matter how great a grudge you bear against someone, do your best to forgive that person while you are still on Earth.

Let's face it, each of us is constantly committing sins, big and small. And if we had to pay others back for all the wrongs done against us, we would have no time for anything else. That's why Christ commanded us to forgive others.

"Forgive them, Father! They don't know what they are doing." (Luke 23:34)

Christ himself was sinless, and yet he refused to hate those who crucified him. He could see the tragic future of their souls and pitied them, praying to God for their forgiveness. Christ showed us the most merciful path a human soul could take, even if their lot was to be murdered. Christ also taught us that being able to forgive would mean much greater grace for us from Heaven. After his crucifixion and resurrection, the disciples Peter and Stephen were able to continue along the path of the cross, forgiving others without fearing death.

The fundamental law of the universe

No life form, particularly human, can sustain itself without conforming to the laws of coexistence. Given that each person is different, in order to coexist it is vitally important that we all recognize and appreciate our differences. And yet all too often people attack others who don't share their opinions. This happens in societies and communities large and small, and in the workplace. And it has been this way since the beginning of time.

Nothing will change as long as humans have free will. Christ knew this even when he commanded us to "love your neighbor" (Matthew 22:37). Many people believe Christ was talking about people near us. But I interpret it to mean that it is important to listen to and understand people who differ from us. I feel that Christ's words were speaking to the most basic principle of the universe: coexistence.

You can almost say that a coexistent conscience is the same as the spirit of love. The universe is aiming for humankind to live together in love despite differences in ideas, attitudes, status, or wealth. And this isn't limited to human beings. Microorganisms, insects, fish, birds, and all life forms fulfill a role in the scheme of things. This is what keeps the ecosystem going. The universe has a need for all forms of life, no matter what the degree of evolution or intelligence.

St. Francis of Assisi (1181–1226) is frequently credited with the following poetic explanation of what loving one's neighbor means:

The Peace Prayer of St. Francis
Lord, make me an instrument of your peace
Where there is hatred,
Let me sow love;
Where there is injury, pardon;
Where there is error, truth;
Where there is doubt, faith;
Where there is despair, hope;
Where there is darkness, light;

And where there is sadness, joy.

O Divine Master grant that I may not so much seek to be consoled
As to console;
To be understood, as to understand;
To be loved, as to love.
For it is in giving that we receive,
It is in pardoning that we are pardoned,
And it is in dying that we are born to eternal life.

Some people who lost family and friends in the terrorism of September 11, 2001, actively opposed the United States' invasions of Iraq and Afghanistan. They didn't want anyone else to suffer the same pain they had. To me this was a true expression of loving one's neighbor. I felt as though they had realized the merciful love Christ taught us when he died on the cross.

"It is in pardoning that we are pardoned" is the true root of neighborly love. It is those who awake to this love and a true understanding of universal coexistence who are able to move from the caterpillar stage and be reborn.

Getting ready for rebirth

In his prayer, St. Francis used the words "eternal life." I believe that the caterpillar's metamorphosis, its rebirth as a beautiful butterfly, accurately mirrors the path to eternal life. But to me being reborn is not what happens after death. In fact, the Bible even says you can't enter the kingdom of Heaven without being reborn. So what does this mean?

First of all, being open to the notion of rebirth depends largely on how you see yourself. Most people think of themselves only as what they have been since birth. But the bodies we are born into are merely temporary vessels. Our bodies and the environments in which we are born are but the materials and place for us to recreate ourselves. We become our true selves, the selves we were meant to be, only after we are reborn. To do this we must throw away our temporary bodies.

The ultimate purpose of every single person on Earth is to evolve into a butterfly. And we all have the capacity to accomplish it. But most people consider their caterpillar selves to be all they will ever have. They spend their entire lives at that stage, mumbling and grumbling as they go.

What must we do to be reborn? When Nicodemus asked this, Christ responded:

> "I am telling you the truth," replied Jesus, "that no one can enter the Kingdom of God without being born of

water and the Spirit. Flesh gives birth to flesh, but the Spirit gives birth to spirit." (John 3:5-6)

"Water" and "the Spirit" are symbolic Biblical expressions. Being reborn with water means having the proper way of thinking and being enlightened to truth. Being reborn in the Spirit means acting in truth—in both your lifestyle and your actions. Swedenborg used the word "reformation" to express being reborn with water. He called being reborn in the Spirit "regeneration."

Being reborn with water represents being enlightened to truth; learning how to distinguish between what is correct and what is not. You could call it a type of ideological reform.

Being reborn with water is the first step, and being reborn of the Spirit is the second. In other words, next we need the power to move, to act. No matter how well we are able to judge right from wrong, it won't come to anything unless we are able to act on it.

It's like reading a book on swimming but never getting into a pool. Just thinking about swimming won't get you anywhere. Until skills are actually used they are useless. And that is what we have human bodies for. Being born again in the Spirit, regeneration, means getting a brand new soul from God—it's not merely a change of heart.

So you see, we receive new lives, first by learning the right way to think, and next by putting those new ideas into action.

To do this, it is important to remember that we all have the evil DNA of our ancestors and we must all repent our sins and become humble. With this in mind, both self-hatred and introspection are opportunities for us to change. Half the battle is having a good conscience that encourages us to leave our evil behind. If we maintain our desire to live with true love within us, we will most certainly continue along the path to accomplishing it.

TRANSLATOR'S NOTE

I was first introduced to Tadahiko Ito's books a couple of years ago, at about the same time another self-help book was selling by the millions in my native United States and other English-speaking countries. Naturally, I was dubious. Was Ito offering something similar? Was he promising the secret to wealth and success? And if I followed his suggestions, would I be the envy of all?

Happily for me and my stalwart Protestant background, the answer was "no." Far from being based on pseudoscience or get-rich-quick schemes, Ito's books essentially champion good common sense. He promises happiness, but it is clear that good fortune and prosperity are not things achieved in a vacuum. In fact, no matter how strongly focused you might be on success, Ito insists that it is equally important to think about your family, your colleagues, even your subordinates.

One might wonder why anything so basic bears repeating. But this is exactly the author's point. Modern society presents us with so many options and possibilities, both positive and negative, that it is easy to get confused. Humankind is in such a state that we need to be reminded of some very simple and basic principles if we want to maintain the world we live in and even dare to dream of personal happiness.

How I Saved a Bank (with a Little Help from the Cosmos) uses a logical line of reasoning, Christian tenets, and the author's wide-reaching experiences in corporate Japan to present a simple set of principles to live by. Ito encourages us to take a step back, take a deep breath, and let a little of that tension out of our shoulders.

As I first read through the books, I could almost see the faces of the account holders when they were informed that the tottering bank was now solid, and that their savings and investments were safe. I thought of the hope small-business owners had been offered; the relief they must have experienced. I was also encouraged to learn that Ito's philosophy on life and deeply held religious beliefs will keep the bank permanently grounded; it isn't going to be a flash-in-the-pan miracle.

In the course of translating these books, I found myself applying Ito's principles to my own life. My family had been going through a series of rough patches, and, as we discussed them over the dinner table, I found I had something new and positive to share. "Well, you know what Mr. Ito would say about this," I'd begin, and everyone would lean forward. We began to look at seemingly hopeless situations in brand-new ways. We discovered that when a little happiness and success are achieved for one of us, it generates joy that supports the rest, and all are encouraged.

Since my family has a Christian background, Ito's suggestions were familiar and easy to accept, and yet there was something new. As the author states, even the words in the Bible mean different things at different points in one's life, and perhaps I was ready to reap the benefits of Ito's long experience applying his Christian principles to his life and work.

Ito goes further, asking us to consider the power of the cosmos and the intentions of the creator of the universe a few steps beyond what we learn in Sunday school. He doesn't demand it; we are free to make our own decisions on the matter. All he asks is that we listen and consider the possibilities. I found them to be exciting and full of hope—and perhaps, not all that difficult to understand.

It has been a joy to have a part in sending this book off into the world in its English version. I hope you have found something that will turn your life in a new direction—maybe in the direction of the cosmos. And once you're in sync with the rest of the universe, who knows what wonderful things can be accomplished!

Deborah Iwabuchi
Maebashi, Japan 2009

(英文版) 宇宙が味方する経営
How I Saved a Bank (With a little help from the Cosmos)

2009年6月25日　第1刷発行

著　者	伊藤忠彦
発行者	富田　充
発行所	講談社インターナショナル株式会社
	〒112-8652　東京都文京区音羽 1-17-14
	電話　03-3944-6493（編集部）
	03-3944-6492（営業部・業務部）
	ホームページ　www.kodansha-intl.com
印刷・製本所	大日本印刷株式会社

落丁本、乱丁本は購入書店名を明記のうえ、講談社インターナショナル業務部宛にお送りください。送料小社負担にてお取替えいたします。なお、この本についてのお問い合わせは、編集部宛にお願いいたします。本書の無断複写（コピー）は著作権法上での例外を除き、禁じられています。

定価はカバーに表示してあります。

© 伊藤忠彦 2009
Printed in Japan
ISBN 978-4-7700-3105-1